Words Of the Past

notionpress.com

Words Of the Past

Deekshit E

notionpress.com

Notion Press

Old No. 38, New No. 6

McNichols Road, Chetpet

Chennai - 600 031

First Published by Notion Press 2016

ISBN 978-93-5206-685-8

If you have a sensitive mind and record your observations regularly, you will see your life too is a vast storehouse of stories.

– Sudha Murthy

"Life means some sort of years, some sort of emotions, some sort of notorious things."

"Behind everything a strange emotional experience will be present."

"Memorizing our past

The only beautiful thing we get from past is 'memories.'"

CONTENTS

ACKNOWLEDGEMENTS

Thanks to

My brother, who always encourages me. When I sounded him out about the book he blessed me with his word. After getting a sense of my passion, he pushed me without saying no.

My mother, who never scolded me even if I wasted time.

My friends Kiddie and Putty, who gave me their best suggestions and they supported me at all stages.

My sisters for being in my life.

To the editor.

Notion Press Private limited, for publishing.

And to dear readers who are going to pull back their past.

PREFACE

"Life means some of years, emotions and notorious things. Behind every notorious thing a strange emotional experience will be present."

"Life is the same for every idiot but how we live our life is quite different."

This is the biography of a person and his past life's experience.

The story is about a twenty-two-year-old guy, who completed his graduation. He doesn't have any sense about his future. He doesn't know what he wants to do and what he wants to become. He is in pell-mell stage. He is critically passionate about creativity. But his studies are different. So he just wasted his time by thinking, thinking, thinking and thinking.

Seasons are changing but he didn't get anything.

Here he gets a sense.

Like others, he has a life too.

Like others, so many notorious things happen in his life.

Like others, he enjoyed his life too.

Like others, he completed his studies.But all this happened in a different angle, not like others.

All of his schoolmates and college mates are running after a salary, but he's not.

His mates enjoyed their life better than him, but one doesn't know how every idiot gets his life. He is poor in enjoyment, but he thinks about his past. He memorizes his past and his lost smile.

He gets more nonsense than others.

He enjoyed his life in between in his own space. His visualization and his sensible thoughts on his past make sense to him. So he decided to make it into a book.

Then he started his nonsense from childhood to engineering.

Here I am expressing about a past and its beauty. And it is about our lost smile.

INTRODUCTION

The story is totally filled with past life experiences. Everyone has a past. Every kid has some notorious thing in his life. From my past twenty-two years, I too have some notorious things.

Life has three seasons.

Past, Present and Future.

We start our life in the present season; when our present moves to future, automatically the present turns to past, and future becomes present. But past never changes its stance.

The only day I am seeing is the present. Past and future are in my thoughts – I'm feeling the past and the future, but I'm not seeing the future and the past.

Lots of naughty stuff happened in my life too.

When I robbed in a fancy store for the first time, it was an awesome experience. But the second time I was caught by the shop owner. That was not a good experience.

My first crush makes me tonsured.

And my second crush makes me breathless.

'Cause of my passion, I learned smoking.

A fearful incident takes me to 81%, this the highest marks in my life.

Curiosity on my third crush sent me to the police station.

I'm too far from girls but too close to crushes.

And malpractices in answer sheets.

At the age of eleven a strange friend entered my life and he made my life dumb. He travelled with me for ten years.

The first time when my dad slapped me, I felt the pain and I got angry too with him. When he slapped me the last time, the very next day he made me sorry too. From the first slap to the last slap, days are changed and emotions are also changed. From angry to sorry, lots have changed. With the rotation of days, lots of things happen. Beyond everything a remarkable lesson, a remarkable happiness, a remarkable naughtiness, a remarkable sadness is present.

CHILDHOOD

4 December 1992 - I don't know how many happiest things and lousy things happened or not on that date. The only happiest thing I know is my birth. After my brother, again a male guy entered into my family. So again all are happy. My birth was not that much an interesting part. A few minutes before my birth, my mom was getting ready to move to the bus station. But my mom moved to the hospital cause of my urgency. At 8 am on 4th December 1992, I entered into this world.

"We do not fall on this earth by sperms; we are here by our loved ones."

Many people are pulling on their burdened lives, weeping.

So like those guys, I also entered the war to fight with the life in this world, crying.

Until I was five years of age, I didn't know that I was also one of the guys surveying this world. A sixty-year-old man remembers his age, but he doesn't remember the sixty years of his history. So my childhood life should be a blurred vision. When I get hungry, I start to cry, after my belly gets relaxed I move to sleep, and a meaningless full laugh for a meaningless full enjoyment… This is my small mellifluous jovial life. Kids don't know smiling and crying, but they laugh and cry louder and bigger. Thus we say that kids are Gods. The only sense they have is reaction - they cry if any one pinches, and they laugh if any one makes them laugh.

Smiling and crying are the sudden surprises for kids.

Slowly I started walking and then I started speaking also. 'Ma, Nana…' I started calling my parents; I do not know how they reacted on hearing my words. But this maturity of mine elicited heavy reaction from them.

Slowly I turned three years old. My brain was getting matured, and ironically my parents' brains also matured a lot. They decided to enroll me in school.

Goddess!

Until now, only my hunger deserved my crying. Now my school also deserved my crying, a three-year-old kid deserves it. But as for me, I didn't deserve it and I didn't like it, and I hated it, only my parent deserved it. From now onwards my environment has changed a bit. Until now I would wake up at any time, but now there was a specified time to rouse me from sleep. My life was too small - just crying, laughing, eating and sleeping; now it turned to crying, crying, and crying. For me, the morning is the laziest time, and the evening is the active time… not only me, every kid doesn't like the morning. Getting up from sleep is the most and most and most…?

So in a week, kids like only Sundays. And Sunday morning is over active time not only for me and for all other kids as well. So Sunday is our day; it's kids' day.

On the first day of my school I cried vigorously, violently. But my mom never heard my cries; she just kicked me to school. After two to three days, my crying has stopped, I don't know why. According to my mom, I just cried only for two to three days, and after that I didn't. How did this happen to me? Till now the only thing that I am aghast at is, how I became addicted to school. When I ask this question to myself it resounds from all sides. That's the only stupendous thing that I didn't get till now. Because I have never liked studies till now, that's why it is a stupendous thing for me. Even if I get a five digit salary for teaching, I will never ever move to schools or colleges for teaching. Because I don't like teaching, studying and books, etc.

I didn't like schooling right from my childhood, but my parents never listened to my crying. I don't know how to express my feelings over than that. Like all other kids, I too cried. Like all other parents, my parents too pushed me into school without understanding my feelings. Slowly I became addicted to it. Every new thing is interesting for kids. But this schooling is not like the others things; slowly, we get addicted.

First we cry to express ourselves, but parents never listen, then the next day and next day we hope to be understood, at last we lose hopes, and then we get addicted to school; it's not addiction really, it's just adjustment to some demands.

Till now this is running, if we want to go we need some demands, if not, we do some rock and roll on roads.

School is a thing that I loathe. This is my opinion on studying.

My childhood schooling means a half day school. In summer times, between the last week of March to the first week of April, we have morning school, as it is the time for public exams for the 10th standard students. Our school was a center for the public examinations. The exam was from 10 am to 12:30 pm. We have a half day, not a half day, it's a quarter day school. The school timings were from 7 am to 10 am. So we would go to school at 7 O' clock with a tiffin carrier in the other hand. At 8:30 we had a tiffin break;

this was the time I liked best. The whole school had their breakfast. It looked like a crowded market. I used to like this noisy crowd. It's just a fifteen minutes break. No fun happens in 15 minutes, it's only a break for hundreds of students. All the ground would be filled with boxes full of tiffin. I used to like this break a lot. Lots of stuff in lots of boxes and having a lump of tiffin from each box… It's a belly full experience for me. I, my brother and my younger sister, we three would take breakfast with my brother's friends. And this was the only time I used to spend with my brother in school. For seven years both of us studied in the same school, but I didn't spend even seventy minutes of my time with him, and I don't remember more than this. In school his work was with his classmates, and my work was with my mates. From the whole of my academic year, this is the time I liked best.

The first thing that happened and the first thing I remember from my childhood…

My grand ma kicked me out of the home, just for a rupee.

Let's move into the story.

One day I cried for a rupee. I saw an ice cream van moving on our street, we used to call it 'pulla ice'; the ice cream is an ice cube dipped in milk and coated with white cream, fixed on to a stick which was so yummy to lick. When licking the ice we feel hmmmmmm yummy, and the cream flows close over our hand and licking our hand hmmmmmm it's so tasty, it can't be expressed. My street friends were tasting the pulla ice. So how could I miss the chance?

I also wanted to lick the pulla ice, so I ran home. I didn't find my ma there, I found my old grandma instead. She was sitting on a cot chewing betel paun.

Ok.

Whoever it may be, first I want the "pulla ice."

I asked for a rupee but my grandma said, "I don't have," but I didn't leave her.

I asked again, she says, "I don't have."

I cried again and again, but her answer is the same.

If kids want anything they work out the plans.

Plan-A, first they ask, if it does not work, they use Plan-B, it is crying. So my first plan failed and I used Plan-B. I started crying but my grandma did not melt.

Like kids, parents also have their plans. First they refuse smoothly, and if it does not work, they also use their Plan-B. It means they give us sudden surprise for our cheeks.

"A chuckling sound on cheek."

"Slapping."

But here my grandma had a little creative bend to her brain. She didn't slap me, she just kicked me out of the house and closed the door, and in a loud voice she said, "Stay out."

Now Plan-C for kids. Tenterhooked!

I stopped crying; I was shocked. I didn't know what to do. Really it was a sudden surprise for me. I missed the "pulla ice" and on top of that I got my grandma angry. Until noon I wandered over the streets. At noon my father came home from the office.

My father was a Central Government employee. He worked in the B.S.N.L. At 7 O' clock in the morning he would go to office, and in the afternoon at 2 O' clock he would return home. So on his return, I went in with my dad.

Someone said that,

"Even a stopped clock can be right twice a day."

– Anonymous

My revenge started:

There came one fine time when my grandma went out for a chit chat with her old tooth less friends. That was my stopped clock. When she returned home I had closed the door.

She asked me to open.

Stay out you three legged old woman, I shouted. Now my old grandma was really surprised, she was shocked and then she laughed.

My dad too was shocked,

"Hey idiot she is my mom, what happened to you, ha. Open the door.."

But I didn't.

He came and opened the door. I was not satisfied.

I gave an angry look at my grandma.

There is a difference between me and my grandma. She knew the meaning of anger even when she got angry with me and kicked me out.

I didn't know why she did that!

I was not at a good age to think why. Only Newton's 3rd law works here. For every action there is an equal and opposite reaction. It works on me. My grandma gets angry on me; eventually I get angry too on her.

Elders show their angry emotions on children. If they get angry with someone or at anything, they show it on others. Nature's true.

But kids are not like that; they show their emotion on the person who makes them angry. So that's why we say that "Kids are creations with chaste minds."

"We find fresh emotion in kids."

Kids are the best examples for emotions……

Days passed. Four years after my birth my grandma expired. The entire family was weeping.

The silent sleep of my grandma takes my family to a sadness-filled silence.

All were wailing. I didn't understand anything. It was a fearful incidence. This was my first fearful incidence at the age of four. My old grandma has passed away.

After years I found that I missed her. We need grandparents; without them a home is nothing. My grandfather passed away before my birth. When I see grandparents walking on roads with their grandsons, I feel a great sadness. At the age of four I lost my grandma. I don't remember her face even; not only me, my grandparents also missed us. Only my elder sister could enjoy my grandpa's money, I and my brother could not.

Having grandparents and scolding them and a pleasant evening walk holding grandpa's last finger, and we do some nonsense with them, it's a good feeling. If our parents get angry on us immediately we hide behind them and they save us from mom's beatings, and if we participate in any street fights before the dad our grandpa will move into the fight with friends' parents. If we score less marks, we are saved by our grandparents from dad's anger. I missed all this fun.

If we do any nonsense, we would get at least a single scolding from dad, but from grandfather, never. We even manage to escape from dad's anger. Mom and dad stay quiet in front of their fathers, but we grandsons have the right from "emotional relation democracy," we have the right to kick, we have the right to fight with them, we have the right to scold them, and we have a right to do any nonsense and even to push our mistakes on to them. If we have grandparents we earn so many chocolates. And we are the only ones in the home who earn better than dad.

Dad is a hero who saves us from all the problems and he stands by our side, and grandfather is our super hero who stands before us and he saves us even from the hero.

Every kid holds his father's finger, but some kids hold their grandfather's finger.

I missed all the fun and my grandparents also.

But a miracle happened - within a year my grandma returned. Another kid entered into my family. It was my sister. We treat her like my old grandma, and she also has a big mouth and a louder voice; if she opens her mouth, she uses only bad words, just like my grandma.

By her entry we turned to four. She has born in Bellary, which is my mom's native place, and is located in the state of Karnataka. My father's native place is Jammalamadugu located in Andhra Pradesh. It's not a love marriage, it's an arranged marriage. Hundreds of miles separate the two families, even though they became together. This we called Brahma's destiny.

I remember her birth; she was born at night. After her entry, my crying slowly stopped. Proudly I transferred it to my sister. Now she started crying. Slowly my parents became indulgent to my sister. If I do anything mischievous, my parents says to my brother, he is a kid ra just leave it, when you are kid you had also done the same as him. And now they are saying it to me.

What a changeover.

My life has started to change.

I had become big; my parents were also transferring their love. Every morning I would take the bath first, but now my sister was taking it first. Before her entry, every day I would take a shower two times. Now only once, I took shower in the morning, and no shower in the evening; and the quantity of milk was also reduced to half a glass. Daily my mom used to come to the school to drop me, now mom handed my hand to my brother.

Oh God!

From now onwards I can't cry on roads, if I do he gets angry, because he is not mom to indulgence. And dad also changed, when he returns from office, he directly goes to see my sister, and catching her in his hands kisses her.

God, all are changing.

Cars and toys grew closer to me, fighting with toys, and playing with street friends, slowly I also changed.

She is taking everything from me.

Yes really she was my old grandma, who had come back to take revenge on me.

INCIDENTS

I HAVE BEATEN MY DAD AND DAD HAS BEATEN ME

When I was a kid I have beaten my dad so many times. If anyone made me cry, the very next minute I would show it on my dad. And my dad would show his reaction on them. I enjoyed it. I learned this from my grandma. I learned this fast. At that time I showed it on my grandma, but now I am showing it on others. This incident spells that I'm growing.

When I was a kid, I was treated as innocent, but now that I was turning big, I started learning cunningness. Countless times more have I beaten my dad, than he beat me. Perhaps he never will break my record. Not only others, I would make him beat my brother also.

One fine day, my brother was playing with his friends. My dad came and said, go and call him. I went and I called him but he was busy with his street mates so he got angry with me, and eventually I too got angry with him.

Ha ha ha!

He didn't know about me, I was growing, so how could I leave him. Then the reaction came from my dad. My dad tore his skin.

Every elder has to understand one thing, in respect of a younger kid; you have to behave properly, if not you will taste fear. The same thing happened to my brother.

No one escaped from my dad; not even me…

Once, at a bad time, my brother, my elder sister and me, we three went to a relative's home to watch a movie.

Here I want say something about my elder sister. During my childhood days, she was with me, but after six to seven years she moved to a hostel and continued her studies far away from home. Every Sunday, mom and I went to the hostel to see her. After completing her schooling she returned home, and thereafter completed her graduation in our town. And later she moved to university for post graduation. So she spent most of the years of her education in the hostel. In my child hood she was close to me, but later she moved away. She was like a guest for me, I would see her only during holidays, and after the holidays, she would again move to the hostel. When I entered the intermediate class, she grew close to me.

More than with me she was very close to my brother.

So the three of us went to watch movie, and it was already 8:30 in the evening. We didn't go home, and we were still at the relative's home. My dad waited and waited for us to come home, until he lost all his patience, and at last he became very angry. His anger was at its peak, and his face had turned red. I don't remember whether he beat my brother or not, but he beat me.

He came and called us.

My brother and my sister went out silently, and at last I came out. I didn't see my dad's face, and I didn't notice anything, I just bent my head and walked silently. But my dad was very angry and gave me a strong heavy blow on my neck. A shrieking voice came out of my mouth.

Ammaaaaaaaaa I cried.

This was the first time, but it was not the last time.

Another incident:

It's a shameful incident, but after it turned to the past, it looks funny. This happened when I was in my 5th class. In the unit test exam I failed in one subject; it's not even a subject, it's our first language TELUGU. From sunrise to sunset we walk on and talk in that language - even then I failed in Telugu. Now this time it was a heavy, heavy blow, not a blow, a slap on my cheek.

"Chipaak."

I'm a kid who was not good kid in studies, I don't know why. It's not my fault, it's Brahma's fault, but no one here is willing to accept it. He wrote all this on my forehead, but everyone is blaming me. Not only from my dad, but also from school, I used to get lots of slaps on my cheeks because of studies. No, I can't say because of studies, it's because of Brahma's fault.

The mistake is made by someone, but we are getting punishment for it. If a student doesn't get good marks, teachers never think why he is not getting the right answers, they just slap him, that's it. I think this is the first rule they learn in training. They treat us as their own kids, just like parents.

God!

From both parents and teachers I'm getting two pairs of slaps. All teachers, parents and neighbors, everybody stands in the same line… they never think.

If we are in a good position everyone says he has good fortune and God wrote good fortune on his forehead, but if we are in a bad position they blame us, not God.

Don't know why?

If we are ready to do a work which we don't know, parents say, "No don't do it, Nana, you don't know about it, you can't face the result." But in studies it's different. If we say that we are not interested in studies, we are passionate about something else, they never listen to our words, and they just kick us into school.

Why do parents behave like this? Who can answer these unanswered questions?

Seeing all this I get a doubt about parents – do parents lose their brains after marriage? Why, because they have experienced this age, and they know everything about it, but they never think.

A kind example – my dad was very passionate about football, he had played football in his school and college times. If a FIFA world cup starts, he sticks to the TV, he doesn't look at his watch, and he doesn't take care about anything else; he just sticks to TV. If a match is held at mid night, he wakes up and watches the match. He is that passionate about the game.

But once, when I asked to buy a football, he scolded me, saying, "Go ra, go and study first."

Why?

What's happened to my dad?

Has anything happened to him after marriage?

They have reached this stage after having crossed our age; even then, they never think.

Why have they changed?

After that first slap, I got more slapping from my dad

But the last time when my dad slapped me, the very next day he said "sorry" to me also.

In between my first slap and the last slap, not only my age, my emotions also changed.

"My dad is my hero and he is my villain."

"When he slaps me he looks like a villain, when he says sorry, he turns to be a hero."

SOME OF THE INCIDENTS WHEN I GOT BLOWS FROM OTHERS

Some of the fellows also beat me…

This incident took place on the Ganapathi festival. On the Ganapathi immersion day we celebrate it like Holi. All were enjoying their day, by sprinkling colors. I didn't have colors. When I went on to the streets, I found everyone sprinkling colors on the others, and in all innocence I asked for colors from one nasty guy. He was already a nasty fellow, so he sprinkled colors in my mouth and ran away; he didn't even give me any colors.

I cried!

I didn't do anything, I ran home with my mouth full of colors.

And mom asked me what had happened. Then she gave work to her own mouth.

She scolded me, not him. "Idiot, while he was sprinkling colors on you, what were you doing? Ha, don't you know to react? Useless fellow, go, go and wash your mouth."

My facial expression had changed. I went to the bathroom to clean up my mouth.

On that same day another nasty experience happened to me.

By this incident I came to know that I can't get my parents.

One of the guys on my street sprinkled colors on me and ran away. But this time I ran behind him to take revenge, I ran on the busy roads, I couldn't catch him, but still I was running behind him like a hungry lion. But just before I could catch him, my brother caught me, pulled me aside and started scolding me. I behaved like as a wrathful fellow.

"He sprinkled color on me, so I have to take revenge on him," I shouted at my brother.

My brother was shocked, "Hey what ra what are you saying?" He asked in a soft voice.

When my brother spoke thus, I was also a bit shocked. Because it's not in my attitude, taking revenge, running behind idiots, that's not in my nature. For me also it was a shocking experience. After this incident I stood in front of the mirror and looked at myself.

During the last incident, I didn't know him, but now I knew that this fellow is a kid from our street. After the last incident mom had scolded me because of my lack of reaction, so now I reacted heavily, and ran behind him.

But whereas mom had scolded me for not reacting, but now my brother was scolding for reacting.

Don't know how to take their words, and not getting how to react.

Don't know why these parents send us into confusion.

And another incident was a truly remarkable incident. And two sub-incidents happened along with this incident. This incident happened on Thursday. I remember the day because my dad brought home mutton on that day. Usually on Thursdays and Saturdays we are far from non-vegetarian. But my dad brought it that day because my cousin had come to visit us. Without saying a word against it, my mom was making it into fry.

My brother, myself and some of my street guys were playing cricket outside. I'm not good at cricket even though I used to play it. I was to bat first. It was the first ball. I missed the ball, and then my friend came and asked me, "Can I play one ball?"

I'm a kind-hearted fellow, so obviously I can't say no, and I gave the bat to him.

He took position and was ready to hit the boundary. It was the first ball and the bowler was my brother; he threw the ball, my friend tried to make hit a boundary and he made it, and with that simultaneously he hit my cheek too.

No sounds from my mouth, I stood silently rubbing my cheek.

"Hoo shit!" He threw the bat and said, "Sorry ra."

I opened mouth to say, "It's ok, ra."

But I couldn't say it. When I opened my mouth, blood flowed out like a flood. My brother ran towards me, but he didn't react as much as I thought he would.

The inner part of my cheek was cut open. I was standing just a single step away from him (leg side of him), so it was not his mistake. My laziness makes me like that. Blood was flowing out of my mouth. If I tried to spit, blood was coming out from my mouth instead of saliva. Everyone came close to check the flow of blood.

The various reactions from them were funny.

My brother and my dad took me to the hospital. The doctor stitched up my lacerations and I returned home.

If anything bad happens we find some link to blame ourselves. My dad bought mutton on Thursday and I'm injured, so thereafter non-vegetarian was strictly prohibited on Thursdays.

But the only thing I was aghast at was, that in our family we are six members, of whom five eat non-veg, but the remaining four were saved, and the only bloody single piece myself, got injured. Why?

All the other four ate mutton and they enjoyed the pieces too. So why did this happen to me?

Before I was born, my mom had prayed to lord Sai Baba, and made a promise not to take non-veg on Thursdays. So mom made a deal with Sai Baba, and for that deal I was the surety. That's the reason the mishap happened to me. This was the explanation I got from my mom.

God!

"Is God also taking interest in crossing rules?"

Mom said, "No, God is the one who punished us."

Whatever it may be, surety gets punishment for the mistakes of borrower.

Here another sub-incident happened. Some of the street friends of my sister were going to a function, so she too wanted to go. When we got back from hospital, my sister started crying. She was then a six-year-old kid. Her crying made her look like a sweet peppered snack.

"Anna, please anna, my friends are going to function anna, and daddy please daddy I want to go." She was crying.

"And anna, they are providing meals also anna, please anna, my friend is going anna, please anna." My brother became stubborn because of her behavior. There was no reaction from my brother, he just stood there surprised.

She was not hearing our words, "Arey chinna, mom made mutton ra, in function you get only rice items ra," my brother was saying.

But she was not convinced; she sat on the floor and was crying for attending the function. She was going on saying the same thing over and over again, and crying, and she was not listening to anybody.

All were laughing at her behavior and me, I just couldn't laugh because I was getting pain; but her crying was a laughable crying.

On the one side the mutton was getting ready, and I couldn't eat it, and I was suffering about the mutton fry, and on the other side my sister was going on crying for the function.

Another sub-incident

For the first time, that day my brother fed me, making me to eat. It was mutton fry; he made me eat mutton fry. At that time it did not seem to be a good time. I kept my attention on chewing the pieces without hurting my lacerations. Now when I think about it, I feel that it was an awesome experience. Now that we are grown up guys having beards and moustaches, when I think about the past, a twinkling laugh sits on my lips. It's an inexpressible scene. It was the first and the last time. After that he never ever made me eat. This happened just once in my twenty-two years.

I don't like him and I like him, he is not a good fellow and he is a good fellow.

He was born before me and reduced my responsibilities. Brahma didn't made any mistake on him.

THE INCIDENTS THAT RESULTED IN MY GETTING BLOWS FROM MY TEACHERS

This incident happened when I was in my 10th class. In this, my friend also took part in scolding me. Me, and my friends Vinod and Dica, we three were fighting, and it was just a fight in jest. Vinod had a strange habit, that whenever he found cheeks, he pinched them. So every time he pinched Dica's cheek, because Dica looked very soft and short. On that day some strange power forced me to pinch his cheek, so I also pinched his cheek; he didn't get irritated. So again that strange power pushed me, I asked once more, he accepted and said ok. But this time Vinod entered and he made it a little nasty. Vinod had an idea. "Arey, I will hold his hands, then you pinch his cheeks ra, it'll be good to see," he said.

I was also impressed on hearing this idea.

"Ok," I said and Dica also accepted,

Vinod tied his hands, and then I pinched Dica's cheek. That's it, the act was completed. But the whole scene was watched by my head mistress, and my HM sent an invitation through the peon. We three went in. My HM was not in a serious mood.

She just asked, "What is going on there?"

We gave an explanation about the incident; even Dica also explained that it was just fun. But a surprise gift was waiting for me. Surprise stood beside my HM in the shape of my sister.

'My sister' came to the HM's room. After hearing our nonsense my HM didn't get angry, but my sister made her get angry? Here my sister showed her enormous affection for me.

She said, "Ma'am, he is my brother please excuse him Ma'am," she requested.

These words made my HM so angry, and immediately my HM got the stick and started beating us. Our butts turned red. Not only from my HM, after that Vinod also showed his enormous anger on me.

Actually my sister needs this special treatment because she entered in between, and at a small age she is recommending for excuses, so she needed it, but here I got the treatment.

What's wrong with her? I went home a little angry with her, but my dad stopped me and asked about the incident. After listening, my dad laughed at me.

And my dad said, "Arey, you can't escape from scolding today, your sister was just a reason, that's all. If she were not there you would have got it because of someone else."

God, both are the same. I went in without changing the expression on my face.

"Even enormous affection is also a danger sometimes."

Another incident:

Now this time it was by Sri. He was my classmate. One day Sri was beaten by my class teacher. My friends laughed at him, he got angry and complained to his mother and then to the class teacher. Next day my class teacher came and asked Sri for the names of those who had teased him, and he gave some names. In that list I was also there. Then again… the fights started.

With or without mistakes from my side, I was getting beatings. Sometimes we escaped after committing mistakes, but sometimes we got caught without any mistakes from our side.

When I was in 9th class, my second crush made me angry too, without any mistake on my side. After that she made me breathless. And I stopped…

Incidents ..

Some incidents are curious and some are not, and some are reasonable and some are not, some are laughable and some are serious, some incidents take time to peak, and some incidents are off within minutes, but after every incident we get something and we find something.

Incidents are a part of life.

Something sticks from every incident.

"For every change a strange incident will take place."

SCHOOLING

"The first indulgence we get only from mom, and the first slap we get from dad. After this our life will start."

My life started.

From my child hood I was not good at studies. At the age of three I joined school. I joined in LKG (lower kinder garden). In the class all were the same as me, all were crying, some stopped crying and were licking chocolates, and some were crying even while licking chocolates. I was also crying, but who was there to listen to my cries. For the first day to about three days, this happened with everyone, and then it become normal to everyone in the class. Every day in the morning I was getting a pocket full of stuff to stop crying. And in the afternoon again I would get some stuff to stop my crying. This continued for a week; after that I stopped crying and I got addicted to school, I got new friends and I showed interest in going to school. Observing this my mom also stopped filling my pocket. And I started adjusting with one chocolate.

In our times we didn't have nursery, so directly I joined in LKG. My subjects were alphabets and numbers – only two subjects. A,B,C,D,E,F,G,H,I,J,K,L…total twenty-six alphabets. Before learning the numbers I learned twenty-six alphabets, and then numbers 1,2,3,4,5,6,7,8,9,10. From my third year onwards I was learning these things, which I didn't like. I completed my LKG with twenty-six alphabets and some numbers and Telugu alphabets.

In LKG my big long sweet name turned to short and sweet. Because of low space in attendance book and even my class teacher also not getting the spelling, so she made it into a short and sweet one. My first academic year in school was completed with alphabets and numbers.

I was promoted to UKG. In LKG we had only morning session. ABCD's in the morning, and sleeping in the afternoon. But in UKG, it is upper kinder garden not like LKG, now we were seniors in school and our younger ones were joining in LKG, so we had full day classes.

A for Apple, B for Ball, C for Cat… we started learning words in the morning session, and the remaining numbers in the afternoon, so no rest. In LKG I had cried for some days and later on I had stopped. In UKG, I didn't cry at all. In the morning my mom used to come with me and drop me at school, and my mom would give me one rupee or half a rupee to make me stop, and these coins were of use in the interval. For kids, coins and chocolates play an important role. In childhood our parents make us corrupted; by giving chocolates and biscuits they tempt us. So obviously we also behave like corrupted and we enjoyed that. But if we behave much more they beat us, they only make us like this and they only beat us while we corrupt more. Mostly we played this act in our school days only. But if we behave like that in adult age, senselessly our parents scold us.

"School days are golden days, we get anything with a simple cry."

If we cry for an elephant, even elephant also come in front of us. Our dad turns to an elephant and we ride on our dad and he gives us a joyful ride.

At kinder garden stage we get anything we want, but when we are promoted class by class, we lose many things one by one.

Like this my school days went on, and next I was promoted to 1st class, then 2nd class, and to 3^{rd}class, and 4th class. I do not remember much about that class. My past is not much clear up to 4th class. Up to the 5th I don't know how I studied, and there is no need to remember also, I know how my marks would be, so no need to memorize. In my progress card, only my mom's sign will be present; my dad never used to sign, because he likes me but he didn't like my 50% marks. But in some rare cases, it means if I cross to 60%, then he would put his sign on the card. And 60% was like a girlfriend to me, don't know when it comes, and don't know for how many days I would carry it. So in every unit test and in final exams I passed with average percentage.

But once, I failed in the final exams; I don't remember in which class it happened, but I failed in the final exams. In our school if anyone failed in final exams, he would be detained, and I had failed in the final exams. And I thought I was going to be sitting in the same class and that they had decided to detain me. After joining in school, this was the first problem I was facing. I didn't know how the situation would be, and how my dad would react, or what he would do after seeing my card. Until that time, I had been a 50% student. But now these final exams threw me away. I didn't know the meaning of breathless but I was breathless with fear. I was just a kid and didn't know how to escape. Fear engulfed me. Then my class teacher entered into the war field to save me. She spoke with the head mistress and saved me from being detained, not only from the detention, but also from the situation which I could not even bear to think about.

From childhood onwards I had been seeing my dad, I had seen his anger and his love, but the only thing I missed that time was his reaction. When I had imagined my failure scene, I couldn't even imagine how his reaction would be. Only that time I missed his reaction.

On that occasion I mentally congratulated my class teacher, but after the moment passed, I noticed that I missed my dad's reaction. If I got low marks he would get angry with me, but I didn't know how angry he would be if I kicked the final exam.

I get a breathless situation, and I escape from that, and I think that I'm safe. But later when I think about these situations after many days, then I notice that I miss an important emotion. .

I'm the only one in my home who faced such strange situations. My brother suffered my dad's blow and my sister also, but they never got blows for low marks. I'm the only one in my home who got blows for all possible reasons.

Some say that I didn't get any blows from my parents and that they brought me up with love. What is in that yaar, you have to experience everything? If you feel it is love then getting blows from parents and the very next moment receiving 'sorry' from our parents then what can we call it? I experienced these things from my parents.

And my class teacher who saved me from hell was named Asha. She was the one who made my long sweet name to short sweet name. She was my class teacher, not only for me, for my brother and for my younger sister as well. I don't have better incidents to remember with Asha ma'am.

After our final exams we got the progress card, but at this time my dad checked my progress card in particular because he wanted to check whether I was promoted or not. After receiving the card I went home and I handed it over to mom and I went to sleep, I didn't wake up till evening. I closed the eyes and I counted the minutes. At noon my dad returned home from office. I didn't think whether my dad looked at my card or not, and I didn't think about his reaction, my only intention was that day had to pass, that's it. I didn't want that, day, I wanted the next.

My dad was too intelligent for me, more over he was my dad and he had been watching me for years, so he could easily understand my acting. However, my promotion to the next class made him silent. So I escaped like that.

My dad prefers scolding to beating. I think nearly four to five times I got beatings. But by my mom never, never scolded me, and she never beat me also, but I was frightened so many times, when she makes her eyes big, the very next second I would close my mouth.

Actually sons are mom's little kids and daughters are dad's kids; from the past century this has been running. Eight years after their marriage my elder sister was born, she was dad's kid, and after me and my brother, another kid was born; she was the last kid and she was also dad's kid. After graduation, my elder sister went out for higher studies. During holidays she would come home and she never woke up at morning hours, she would arise only after 10 o'clock, and, if my mom tried to wake her up, immediately my dad would enter the scene and scold my mom, "What are you doing, why are you making her get up? She finds college so stressful, and she comes here for relief. Holidays are only for relaxing not for working, but here you also making her stressed, go, go and do your work." My dad would shout like this.

But if mom's kids sleep till 9 o' clock, there is a slight expression change in his face. This small thing tells about the affection of a father for his daughter.

He shows the same affection to my younger sister also. Actually parents shower their entire affection on the last kids, and if this last kid is a girl then she will be the luckiest in the family. My younger sister is so lucky in that. My dad's affection for her is so endearing.

A small incident... My younger sister is so passionate about eating, she likes eating, eating and eating. Every day a big fight would take place between me and my sister during eating. She needs the whole of her favorite items, and she wouldn't give me even a bite. And my dad also would support her. My dad also behaves like her. If he brings anything he keeps it in the locker because of me, and he gives it to my sister when I'm not at home. Major parts of my dad's coins are used up by my sister only. If I ask for coins for chocolate or for anything he gives me, but if she asks, he gives coins and he brings the stuff also. Why is it that all dads are so kind towards their daughters?

-:-:-:-

So exams were completed and next came the summer holidays. Hoooo huuuuuu...

I like holidays more than ever, not only me, every idiot likes holidays, and in that summer holidays... God! Super, we get forty-five days holidays. And for me summer holidays are more enjoyable days as I'm free from school, no hesitation in the morning, and I can wake up at any time, and no teachers, no books, no stick, no marks, no beatings, no progress card, and totally no peevishness. And I am getting relaxation from the troubles of the past ten and odd months.

During the holiday's mom, my younger sister, and I moved to Anantapur where my aunt lives. I have a cousin, cousin from Bellary who is a different type. We discussed everything between ourselves except my personals. I never shared my personals with him. By age he is bigger than me, but in relation he is equal to me, a very neat and good guy he is, the only good one among all my cousins.

When he was in kindergarten stage, he lived in Bellary, but later on after some emotional situations he came to our aunt's house to continue his studies. He is my guide, not like a spiritual guide. He is too emotional in his relations. In my life two persons have played important roles, and he is one of these guys. At the age of ten I followed his footsteps. The only enjoyment I got in my aunt's house was when I was with him and because of him.

-:--:--:-

Kids react according to their emotions.

When I was at the age of six or seven, I didn't remember exactly at what age I was, on that time I got angry with one of my cousins. This happened when we were at my aunt's place. Before they came to the city, they lived in a village. So mom and my brother, all of us had gone. On some rare occasions my brother also came with us. At that time he came with us.

One day we both went to the railway station. It was a small village, so no express trains stopped there, only passenger trains had a stop there. In a village the railway station looks as peaceful and calm. The railway station was at the center, and on one side of it the village was located, and on the other side there were trees, fields and crops. In a village we don't see any lavatory so for that purpose too we had to move to the other side of the station. In towns and cities we don't see any open lavatories; only in villages we find the outside lavatory. We use the spacious greenery for this. The outside lavatory will be the same as a personal bathroom. In our personal bathroom we are surrounded by walls on the four sides; likewise here also we are surrounded on the four sides by empty greenery, and it's a little different experience.

In morning times the railway station looked a little crowded, as people from the village came to the station and waited for the passenger train to go to other villages for work, or to visit some relatives' homes. We didn't find any heavy crowd as well; it was a peaceful and pleasant place. And it was a place for all the homeless. And a spacious place to play also. When a train arrived, we ran along with the train.

In my childhood, the train was a strange thing for me; it was like an amazing big vehicle for me. In our town we didn't have a railway station, so I hadn't seen that as well. So when I went to that place I felt very happy, and if I travelled on a train I felt very grand, and I boasted to my school mates about that. It was a very awesome feeling for me.

So we both went to the station after our breakfast. Not only passenger trains, some goods train also stopped there. The goods trains however stopped there only if there was another train on the line beyond, which had to cross this station. At that time a goods train was stopped at the station, and we had to go to other side of the track. It was not a passenger train in which we could get in and move out from the door on the other side. Goods trains don't have doors, so how could we go on the other side? My brother went and asked the station master, "Sir, how much time does it take for this train to start?"

He said, "It takes a quarter of an hour."

Then my brother made a plan that to cross the goods train, we had to pass under the train's bogie. This was the plan.

So we passed under the bogie safely and reached the next platform.

After a while my cousin entered; actually he was searching for us, and found us in the railway station. He came in and he was in a serious mood; he asked how we reached that side.

I explained as if it was nothing unusual.

He slapped me.

Tears welled up in my eyes.

What had I done, I didn't do anything, I had come here to play, but he slapped me, and the plan for crossing the train in any case was made by my brother, but he escaped because he was older in age.

I got angry with him, and from then onwards I started hating him.

What he had done was right, the next time I will not do this type of nonsense, but still I was angry with him.

Why should I want to understand this?

"Children never understand the things; they just react according to the emotions. So that's why in childhood times we get lots of slaps on our cheeks, only pain gives us answers".

That time I didn't understand the situation; I got a pain, so I got angry with him, but from then onwards, I never did that type of nonsense.

Every holiday I enjoyed more than the previous one. But the biggest problem I had was with the holidays ending and re opening of the school.

Before my holidays ended, we went back to our town. I hated returning.

Again the same routine days, routine subjects, routine work, routine routine.

In festival seasons also we used to move to our aunt's house. On returning an unpleasant incident happens to me every time, but it does not happen in summer holidays, because in summer we would go back home one week before the school reopened.

But at every festival season this incident happens. After the festival, the next day morning at 5 O' clock we return from our aunt's house by bus. We arrive at 8:30 am. Our school starts at 8:45 am. So my mom's intention is that she wants to send us to school. So we eat our breakfast during the journey itself. So I didn't get any chance to waste time in the name of breakfast and I didn't have a chance to escape also. Before our school timing we had arrived in the town. After getting out from the bus my mom ran like an athlete, holding my sister in one hand and luggage in the other hand. My sister also moved her feet fast; she was a school kid and she treated school as her second home. And me, I was walking ten to twenty feet behind them, slowly, putting one foot after the other foot, like a drunken fellow.. I was not ready to go to school, we were just returning to town, some sleep is needed, but my mom, noooo, she ran back and held my hand and dragged me like a buffalo.

"Come fast, time is running, come idiot."

As for me, I wanted to run away after biting mom's hand, but it was not possible. I went to school weeping.

Why do moms behave like this, if they travel they take some rest, but they never think about us. They behave more perfectly than kids.

I don't have enough brains to escape from this. I'm not a good fox to escape.

It doesn't mean that I'm a domestic fellow. Just that I'm not a well skilled fox at those times.

Don't know that why lots of boys hate school more than girls.

It was the same in my home also; my elder sister was so interested in studies, and my younger one… Oh God! No words will be sufficient to talk about her interest. And my brother is a little irregular in studies, and me, there are no words to say about my irregularity in studies.

Boys show less interest in studies, but in extracurricular activities they show their extra.

Up to my 5th standard my problems in studies moved softly but after that it turned a little rough. Until now my teachers gave us only progress cards. After that they started giving answer sheets also and asked us to get a parent's signature on the answer sheets.

God!

Getting a signature on the progress card was itself a tough job, but now on I had to get the signature on these papers also. It will not happen. I didn't know how to react to this problem.

Day by day teachers were also turning into villains. If we are not good at any subject, they would scold us, and over and above that they want us to get scolded by parents also. Already because of the progress card I was getting heavy treatment at home, now with these papers, I would get double coating.

"My real school life has started from now.

From now my problems are started too

And my nonsense also started.

Where the problems have started there our real enjoyment starts."

2003–2004

6TH CLASS

I entered into sixth standard.

The first and major change from sixth standard onwards is in dressing. From now onwards we were treated as grown up kids, from now onwards we had to wear pants and we kicked away our shorts, we were grown up kids.

"It's so much pleasure to us, to see how we look in pants."

For the first time I wore pants in the fifth class on the occasion of the festival, that was the only pants I had, but from now onwards I wore only pants and not shorts.

"Pants turned to our regular fits."

Wearing pant is a little pleasurable feeling for me, tucking in the shirt, and with shiny shoes for feet a cute dressing sense. It looks very pretty to see my looks in the mirror.

And second major change.

Our teacher asked us to get a sign on answer sheets also.

God, what a change for the worse, how can I make it, it's not a possible thing.

I did not know how to get a signature on the progress card, but from this time onwards, I had to get even on answer sheets also. Hoo God, what the hell is this, at such a small age I have to face so many odds. Is it necessary for me?

Till now my bad luck came irregularly, but now it seemed to stay with me, I didn't know how to kick it off.

My ears started shivering not knowing how to escape from my dad's scolding, and my cheeks didn't know how to cover themselves from getting slapped, my eyes didn't know how to face my dad's angry emotion. All parts of my body were getting tense. Because from now I get everything in twice, God I cried,

After all this we got a unit test, same average routine marks. My teachers gave me my answer sheets; this was the first time I was taking it home and to hell with this new rule. It was a new rule so I didn't do any malpractice. Before the cyclone we get heavy winds to warn us, like that I too was getting forewarned before the finals. On seeing answer sheets my dad make a note with a single line dialogue, "Arey from now onwards don't show your progress card to me again and your answer sheets also," he said.

Hoo that's it. What a cool answer from him, it's too fine for me also.

No slapping on cheeks,

No scolding,

No anger.

And no nothing, I danced on the floor.

From that time my card did not have the luck to get my dad's signature.

Ok fine, nothing happens, and my card was not worrying about my dad's signature; it just needs a signature, from whomever it may be, whether it is by my mom or by my dad, just it needs a signature. So too my answer sheets also.

My marks congratulated me,

From then onwards I went directly to my mom to get a sign.

No scolding,

No fear.

But even then scolding's were not far from me, because of my sister. My brother and my younger sister also studied in the same school. The year I entered into sixth standard my brother left the school. He had completed his schooling. With him I didn't have any problem. But a problem was there by my side in the form of my sister.

So when my sister showed her progress card, eventually my dad looked at me with a shady expression, which means he is a little angry with me. Not only because of my sister. Even because of mom also, if I show my papers to her she says go and show it to your dad.

God, my dad has already told me not to show it to him, but my mom pushes me in to war. Again I stood in front of my dad with the card. He looked at me and he looked at my card, and he repeats the same dialogue. And mom signed on the card.

My mom has a right to keep her signature in the card but even she pushed.

I asked why, and then she said it was respect.

My sisters and my brother were all good at their studies. So every time my younger sister showed her card proudly, but I could not. I would show it to mom and get her signature, my sister would get regards and I would get scolding.

I don't know whether they liked studies or not but they studied well. If they didn't get good marks they felt bad and they take it very serious. Why do they feel guilty? Whether for marks or for sympathy or for any prestige, they can't accept scolding.

I'm not good in studies, so for that reason I get poor marks. If I didn't get good marks I never feel bad, I felt bad only for getting scolding.

My sisters and my brother used to get good marks. If they get 80%, in that 60% is for their interest in studies, and the remaining 20% for fear or for prestige. But for me, I get 50% only for myself. Here no fear, no guilt and no prestige, I'm an average guy, I get what I want. I'm what I am. This 50% is my marks, only my marks. And when I got scolded, I didn't want to care about that, because I want to be as I am, this is my stuff, this is the interest I have. If I bother above feelings, I too am a good kid.

"The duller can study better than the clever. But the only problem is we never realize it."

During my schooling I realized one thing; that no brothers and sisters should study in the same school. It's the most worst horrible thing that we ever have to face. We lost our privacy. We get so many problems because of no mistakes on our part and even when we haven't done any mistakes also. In that respect my elder sister was on the safe side, she studied in another school. But for me it was like being a sheep in a farm. Don't know at what time I will be going to be fry.

After my fifth standard, my brother left the school, so I didn't get any problem from him. He was good at studies. No problem with him, actually no younger gets a problem from elders. Only elders get problems because of younger ones. He didn't get any problem from me and by younger sister also he didn't get any problem, but I faced so many problems, so many shameful days due to my younger sister.

My sister!

From my sixth standard onwards my same full days started. After our unit test exams our class teachers produced our progress cards in the class rooms. But for the rank holders our head mistress produced progress cards in the prayer hall in front of all the students (of the school). Here I got a problem, because my younger sister was a rank holder, and lots of times she used to get her progress card before the whole school in the prayer hall from the hands of my head mistress. In the prayer hall when my head mistress called out her name, she would run swiftly to get her card; her getting a rank was not a problem for me, but the problem was from my mates, all my idiotic friends would look at me while my sister was running to take her card. And I, in the class room I would take my card with average percentage, and sometimes would get beatings also. Really it's the worst time for a brother. A brother like me only can understand these feelings.

..............shit..............

At such times I would scold myself very very badly and very sadly.

Once my dad scolded me badly because of my marks, then my brother entered into the conversation and said, "Dad we didn't take any interest in him, we didn't see whether he was studying or not, and at last when you see his marks you get all fired up, it's not the correct way, dad."

I was surprised, I thought that he was saving me from dad's anger, but later I get it that he pushed me into a problem.

Listening to this, my dad decided to join me in tuition and he threw me into it. And that was the first time I stepped into the tuition.

Going to school is the worst thing for me and now tuition too. What I had done in school, the same thing I would do in the tuition as well. At home I never opened my bag and I didn't take home work also, so my dad pushed me into tuition. I don't know what my dad thought, but if a place changes, nothing will change.

Because of my brother I was going to tuition. I scolded him lots of times.

The tuition was just like me, it looked like my shadow.

My tuition sir was good in his subject. But he ignored me, and eventually I also ignored him. No studying, just going to tuition and coming back to home, daily routine work for me. At my sixth final exams I got 55%. When I showed it to my tuition teacher he asked, "Arey have you improved well here?"

"Ya sir I improved well," I cried.

He felt very happy on hearing my words. On some rare occasions he asks, no it's not asking, he requests me, "Arey, ask some doubts ra; don't sit like an egg ra." My tuition sir begged me so many times, but I never asked even a single doubt.

I didn't have any doubts, so how could I? He didn't understand my intelligence.

Only two categories of people never ask doubts, one is the well known, well educated guys and the other one is the well unknown guys. I don't know which category I belong to.

What is a doubt and why should I want to ask doubts?

When my mates asked doubts I looked at them in surprise. Why are these fellows asking doubts and how can they get doubts? Really these are question marks for me.

I have my ability for 50%, it's enough for me.

So successfully I completed my sixth standard and was promoted to the seventh.

And now I was entering the crucial class.

2004–2005

7TH CLASS

This is a danger zone. Like in the 10th, in the 7th standard also we had public exams. So it was not easy, no Asha teacher was here to help me, even my school teachers were not there to correct our papers. Our exam answer sheets would go to another district for correction. So I had to study, no excuse, no help and no more options. I had to study, I had to get on this.

Rather than me, my dad understands this better.

He started enquiries about good tutorials. And at last he found one. It was my class teacher's tutorial. I joined there.

He was my second favorite teacher. And my first favorite teacher was Asha madam.

This tuition was not like the earlier one. Here my tuition teacher encouraged me a lot; he pushed me up to 60+ percentages. He encouraged me by giving gifts. If I got good marks in slip test he surprised me with gifts. I improved a little, my marks also improved from 50 to 60%. I was so happy, my dad too was happy. Finally my dad concluded that I'm also a stuffed piece. The only thing I need is pushing and a little self-motivation. In the previous exams, if I got less mark my dad scolded me, I think he didn't get an idea to push me. Now here my teacher made this effort, and he succeeded.

My dad made his sign in my progress card.

In earlier classes also he had put his signature in my card, but now he signed with a little happiness, because something had changed in me. From now it turned to a regular thing with him.

I started studying; before that my class teacher pushed me. This was my best tuition, "Here I learned the way of learning." Slowly I turned to above average. Some little changes occurred in this year. A little bit more to study, a bit more confidence. From here I progressed.

About him. He was good, too good a teacher. He was the best example for teachers; in my opinion no other teachers crossed him. A perfectionist, and responsible… He knew how to handle the students, and he knew how to encourage. I can say emphatically that he was the only one who shaped me up. I learned because of him. The increased 10% in my marks happened only because of him.

Slowly my year came to an end. Before the final exams my teachers and my headmistress explained about the public exam. This was our first public exam. Our teachers said, "Don't worry, nothing is going to happen, you guys just have to write in good hand writing, and no rewriting in your answer sheets. If you make any rewritings in your answer sheets, it creates a bad impression; the person who corrects your paper understands that you made a mistake, so you have a chance to get low marks. So please don't do that type of mistakes, if you made any mistake, don't rewrite on it, just leave it, nothing is going to happen, because the evaluator never reads your answers, he just looks to see whether your answer sheet is clean, neat or not. So make your answer sheets clean and neat and make some decoration on your answer sheets, it gives a good impression, and most important thing is good hand writing."

These words our teachers spoke before the exams. Every teacher was saying like this, with some changes and especially about handwriting. No one said study well and give appropriate answer, work hard, no one spelled like that, all my teachers were in the same line. And my teachers said a funniest thing about the evaluators, that is, they will correct your paper in a neat way if they are in good mood, that means if they didn't fight with their wives before coming to the evaluation you will get good marks, if not they will show their anger on your papers.

And after all this, 7th exams are easy. In the previous years it had importance. At the time of my dad's education, 7th was crucial because in those times they were getting jobs after completing 7th. But nowadays it does not have that much importance; two years from my 7th, it was removed from public exams and was treated like any other standard.

Hearing my teachers' words the only thing I got was that I had to present good hand writing and make good decoration.

Days passed and stopped at the final exams, and finally I was at the final exams. I attempted well in the exams and I expected 70% marks. I was a little confident. My public exam was over. After a month my results also were announced. I went to the school to know my results. On seeing my marks I went into shock. I made it! I had got 465 marks, which meant 77%. I ran home to share my 77% of happiness, but my dad was with 33% of anger. He needs some more marks.

Not only kids, even parents also try to rope the sky, the result depends on the work, and the work on the effort. I had just started studying slowly, and it takes time to catch the sky. In some situation parents also behave like kids. But anyways these were my highest marks. I also have stuff in studies, the only need is pushing.

For the first time in my life I learned the work which I didn't know, and which I couldn't.

In the seventh class I changed a little bit; until now I was dumb, my class teacher and my dad make me into some shape. They molded me.

By birth some are good at grasping and some are dumb, but all are good in studies; the only thing is we have to find the way and someone has to push like my dad and my class teacher.

Another good thing that happened when I was in the 7th class was that we built a house. Until then, we had lived in a small hut. Now we moved to a big house. When we were in the hut it was quite good in the hot and foggy seasons, but in the rainy season it seemed like a floating pool. From every sides of the roof rain water entered the house. At night it got to be a little worse, we placed buckets and tubs. And we couldn't even sleep too. And now we built a house, we were entering into that.

We were most happy.

On the opening ceremony of my house we made a puja. For puja there is no use of a younger son. But I was doing too much running this side and that side, then my brother stopped me and said, "Arey what are you doing here, you have unit test exam, go and study and don't do over acting here."

"No ra mom told me to do all these," I replied.

"Go, first go and study," he said in a louder voice.

At that time I had unit exams, but the house was full of relatives. I didn't study anything and in the morning the house was full of sounds with pujas and with relatives, so how could I study? But I had an exam and I didn't have the time to read and to memorize, so I decided to write slip. For the first time I was writing the slip. I opened the book and searched for the questions. I was stunned while searching. For the unit test we have only three to four chapters for the exam, and I didn't know which one was important and which was not. So which one did I have to write, all questions were tempting me, and I didn't have time to write all questions. If I wrote all the questions I wouldn't get a chance to open the slip and to check the questions in the exam hall.

What a bloody fool I am; I didn't even know the important questions, that's why we have to be alert in the class room.

At last I wrote some questions but not being bold enough, I tore the slip. I'm not the gutsy guy, because to do a mistake we need guts too.

And one more incident, a shameful incident for me, on the opening ceremony we had a function. In the evening some of my friends came to my home, I didn't call them but even then they came. But I sent them home, I said to them, "Arey I'll give a party ra, now you guys move from here ra." When I said this to them, without questioning they went back. Why I behaved like that, due to immaturity or due to pride or arrogance, whatever it may be called, I sent them home, which was the worst thing I had done. At that time I didn't realize what I had done. After that one of my friends invited me for their house opening, and I didn't went to the function, but not with any realization. Until then also I hadn't realized my mistake, but after that one of my friends spoke in front of me about the function and about arrogance.

I realized then because I also behaved same. That I had disgraced them, but these idiots never blamed me and they never spoke about my arrogance.

Now I realize that I didn't even call them, but yet they had come, but I behaved rudely, I didn't give them even a cup of tea also. And I didn't give a party also. How and why did I behave like that?

Pity of my attitude,

Shit of my behavior,

We have to know our mistakes by ourselves.

Then only we realize, by this incident I found my mistake.

But no one blamed me, no one pointed out my mistake. Blaming us for our mistake is not a fair way to make us realize it, making us realize by ourselves is a better way.

By this incident I learned something and I got something.

The last days of my 7th class had arrived. Due to some bad communication between relatives, my dad got some problems. We get so many things from relatives, but along with those things my dad got sadness also. Whatever may be the reason my dad lost his respect because of relatives. From our younger ones, we may get problems or responsibilities. My dad got both; at his earning stage he got responsibilities, and now afterwards at the retirement stage he got problems from his younger ones.

The major cause for the problems is 'thinking' and 'understanding.'

"If we say 'think' about the condition, they never 'understand;' if we say 'understand' the situation they never 'think' about the future."

2005–2006

8TH CLASS

Until now my "halo" was small.

I'm not good at playing,

I didn't wander on roads,

I don't move to friend's house.

During the weekends I do only one thing, which is watching television, that's it. I stick to TV on holidays. TV sticks to me, that's the only work I do in holidays.

On rare occasions I play cricket, that also I played in my street and I didn't move far from home.

When I was in the 6th class, I think, my dad said, "Arey nana don't waste your time by watching TV, go out and play something," and he used one proverb also, "A boy will be spoiled without roaming and a girl will be spoiled by roaming."

I liked the proverb and I was impressed also. After listening to his words, one fine morning after my breakfast I went to my friend's house, and till noon I stayed there. My mom started searching for me, because without giving any intimation I had gone out, so she didn't know where I had gone. After a couple of hours I came back. And both my mom and dad started scolding. I just stayed calm, but they were not stopping. After a while I opened my mouth and said, "Dad, yesterday you only said to me 'don't stay at home, you will be spoiled, go out and chill with friends,' so that's why I moved out, now why are you scolding." Hearing this, my mom slowly turned her head to my dad's side, and again mom started scolding, but not me, this time she was scolding my dad.

My dad was shocked and surprised at my words and from that day he never said any proverbs to me, and never told me to go out.

When my mom has a right to sign on my card, even then she didn't do it, she pushed me to take dad's permission, and it was called respect. Now my mom was scolding my dad, and my dad was giving explanations for his fault like a kid, and he was not getting angry with mom. At the age of thirteen my mom got married. Before that they didn't know each other, but after the marriage they started loving each other and respecting each other. And my dad was getting punishment, even then he was silent, and this is called love.

After this incident I also decided not to go to friends' homes because I also experienced an unwanted thing in my friend's home. For the first time I went to Vinod's home and there I spent a little time chatting with him. After a while Vinod's mom came from outside and we stopped our conversation. After some time aunty started chatting with me and slowly the topic went to studies. Shit, everywhere with every person the problem we get is studies. Aunty started asking about the studies, how my studies were going on, and how Vinod was studying, and she went on asking about all this. After a few minutes aunty said, "Go guys, go and study something."

What is happening and this fellow went in and brought the books and he gave me too I started worrying, even in my home also I never used books, but here I was and I decided to run. But I didn't do that, and after a quarter of an hour, aunty took the book and started asking questions.

I was stunned! God! Damn!

Even my dad hadn't asked any questions till now.

What is this and aunty was asking me also?

What?

I didn't give any answers; aunty looked at me violently, I looked at Vinod's face, innocently he also looked at me, and after a while I ran out from there. While running to home once again I memorized proverb which my dad said. From then I decided not to go to friends' homes.

God, I escaped from hell, why do these parents behave like this, every time they say study, study and study?

After this incident I decided home is the best place and TV is best friend. Mom never asked questions and with TV we never get bored. So home is the best place during holidays. Running to friend's home and getting surprise gifts is not fair.

From childhood I was a reserved kid. I didn't move out of my home, and I was addicted to TV.

And some of the reasons for my not going out are:

1. My brother, he entered the world earlier than me. When I went out with him, he hesitated to take me along, he needed some joyful space. Not only he, but also everyone in my family behaved the same. Everyone needs some space. I also behave in the same way as my brother.

In some cases, for example, if I went out to play cricket with him, he would bowl slowly; yes I agree I am not good at cricket, and I'm his brother, so it doesn't mean that to bowl slowly, he has to make me good. But he didn't do like that and he treats me like as kid. I didn't like this, every elder one behaves like this, he wants me to play well, but for me I want to play, I want to learn well. With our street mates we both have good relations; of course he has better equations than me. If they went out to play I also moved with them, but this fellow also comes with us and he fires me. And I would go back home. I went with them only if he was not there, then only I played cricket with them. If he was present, he would treat me like a kid.

I hated this behavior in him. Actually I didn't like it. In our street he made good bowlers and good batters, so many trained under his guidance but he never made me a good player. I never played a single match in his team too

So guys don't make your brother or sisters to play well, make them to play, treat them like friends and don't hesitate when they come with you and don't show your kindness. So guys feel some responsibility in their career, not in enjoyment.

He is one of the accused.

Another reason is my mom. If we moved out for an hour without any intimation she starts searching and crying. If we move out at all, then we had to get back as early as possible. If not then my mom starts crying and searching.

One day I went out for swimming with one of my street guys and I didn't reach home within time, and my mom started weeping. She started running on streets to find me. On returning home I found that my mom was crying.

Hoo goddess!

What's wrong with mom? If she behaves like this, how can a kid learn new things?

Beyond an hour we can't survive, more than me my brother faced this so many times.

If parents have to show enormous love for their kids, I'm ok with that. Even we need that, but it needs some commas. If they never make commas kids put full stop to enjoyment.

And my mom is the second accused.

And another reason is my eye-sight. I don't know the year, I think it was 2002, when I got spectacles. From then my life was drowned. Actually I'm reserved, and now with these spectacles I switched off the enjoyment. Totally my happiness went off.

For nearly ten years I travelled with spectacles. I lost so many spectacles, while playing I split them countless times. In B.Tech third year I kicked it with a surgery.

I can't do anything without spectacles. Day by day my short sight also increased and day by day my problem also increased, from normal glasses to magnifier lens. Earlier I used my glasses only at study time, and I wandered over streets without glasses; afterwards I used it for wandering also, and after that I used it all the time during the day. When I closed my eyes I placed it aside, when I opened my eyes, I searched for glasses; that mean I used my glasses up to the time I slept, and in case I woke up at mid night for water, first I had to wear the glasses, without that I couldn't manage, even if I wanted a good vision in my dream I have to wear it.

Without spectacles even a ghost also can't frighten me.

That much sight I have.

Because of spectacles, I lost important things in life. We are not here just to do some work and earn some food and at last to die, we are here to have some fun also. That fun I missed because of these spectacles. If I removed my glasses I couldn't even find a person, so how can I enjoy with that? If I tried to enjoy wearing spectacles, already I split so many glasses while playing, so I stopped enjoying. Spectacles killed my confidence. My spectacles kicked my happiness.

Spectacles are like a ghost for me, it possessed me, ten years it sat on my happiness. I'm not the single one in the world who having spectacles but it made me empty.

This reason played a key role in my life. So this reason made me dull and dumb. My brother, my mom, spectacles and my reserved nature, all played with me.

"Important years of my life have expired for silly reasons."

With these types of reasons I stopped chilling with enjoyment.

So I became addicted to TV.

TV was my remedy. It impressed me lot. First time when my dad bought TV, I was surprised. And I was so curious to watch it. When I got the first blow on my neck because of watching TV late at night, it made my dad feel bad. So immediately he bought the TV, a 21 inches big TV. Our TV was the biggest color TV on our street, and lots of audience came to our home to watch on Sundays. On Sundays our home looked like a mini theater.

"Watching TV and playing with remote was my holiday time pass."

In the seventh standard I learned something, but here in the eighth, I learned more and I got more. Here I found some more remedies, no it's not remedies, I found enjoyment. I found what I was searching for. Without moving out we can't find anything.

Until now I was like a frog in a well, now I entered into a lake of kilometers of water. Just imagine how deep it would be. So many fishes are swimming in that, some beautiful fishes and some untidy fishes and some naughty fishes and some cunning fishes, but every fish is important to fill the lake.

I started enjoying, I started running and I learned little nasty things. Times pass, robbery in fancy stores, malpractices in exams… Lots of fun I learned here.

Here I learned the meaning of STYLE, CRUSH, and INFATUATION.

In eighth we had a good class teacher and he ran tuitions also. At the start, my studies were not bad. After the seventh, my seventh class teacher left from school. And my studies were not too good. So I decided to join the tuition. And lastly I joined my class teacher's tuition. My classmates were also going to the same tuition. My best time started from here. In the evening after school my friends and I went to tuition on a bicycle, and awesome experience started.

Going to tuition with friends on cycle and making some nonsense, I miss all this fun. And now I'm recollecting it. In tuition studies were nil, enjoyment was full, and in that we had an interval also. One hour after my tuition started we took an interval. We would go out and have a Rayalaseema snack called 'guntha ponganalu' with red chutney. Awesome snack we had during the interval.

An old grandma used to make this snack item. 'Guntha ponganalu' with onion chutney, the taste was so lip-licking, no restaurant could beat this evening snack. We had a great time there. Sometimes we didn't give money also. We confused her with our words. Actually we spent most of the good times in break time only, rather than in tuition.

Lots of comedies used to happen in the interval. After the break we spent little time in tuition and we moved home. At 8 o clock we went back home.

There was a scary fellow also in our gang. We made him frightened every time. He behaved like an exorcist when he was with us. But when he was alone his shadow also scared him. Sometimes we made him cry also.

After days passed, we got a unit test exam. After the seventh I went down to 55 percent. Easily I could bounce back to 60% and I had strength to motivate myself, but my enjoyment dominated my studies. And here I found another way to get good marks. That is by malpractice. It is a simple and easy way to get good marks in the progress card.

Like me my gang also needed good marks but I never made any plans to do malpractice, because my gang was there, and they also wanted good marks. So for me necessary is not required. If we get unfair marks we can't change it on answer sheets, we have to change it on marks list book, and by changing in marks list book automatically marks get changed in the progress card because first our marks were entered in to marks list book so after that the marks in the marks list book are entered into the progress card. So we had to work out our plan. Already we were grown up kids, so signatures in answer sheets was not a problem for me and it's not a tough subject also. So before entering the marks into the progress card we had to overwrite our marks. So the only option, only hope, was that marks list book. We had to steal it, and we wanted to overwrite on it.

First our marks were entered into the marks list book, after that the marks would be entered into the progress card. So before entering it into card I wanted to steal and over write on it. Our class teacher had this marks list book. We all went to his tuition, so during tuition only we had to steal it, and it was the only perfect time to do it. In school no malpractices can be done and it's not easy also. So we decided to do it in tuition, but here a mild problem was there. The problem is grandpa. My class teacher's father… a little risk to overcome this problem, but we were desperate and we wanted to do it. In some situations we can't, in some situation we can. Whatever may be the situation we had to do it.

Plans, cunning, these are our weapons to achieve, and at last we made it. From now I started doing malpractices. In comparison to the student, no teacher is cunning; even if we get caught we search for another way to get marks. We are hopefuls, so our wishes never end, so our cunning plans also never stopped.

Really students are intelligent fellows; if they made a plan every teacher went into shock. If we got caught, immediately we made another plan to escape, but we never used this intelligence on studies.

From now onwards I went in for malpractice. For quarterly and half yearly exams we got question papers from the government, it means government issues the question papers. So after the evening tuition we all ran around for question papers. Till 9 O' clock we ran on the roads, to all sorts of secret places we ran, we didn't know whether we would get it or not but we tried for that. In some places we got some questions for the next exam also, we didn't know that these were the exact questions or not, but we took them serious and we studied because we didn't want to miss a chance. In lucky times we found those leaked questions in the question paper, and if I got those questions I felt happy. But if I didn't get leaked questions in the question paper, it was another differ experience.

But totally the experience was a very good experience, running for questions papers, eagerly waiting for the questions, if we got the questions then we start fighting on night outs, and some wrote slips. On the next day if we didn't get those questions in the question paper then we were on tenterhooks. And then we searched for our nearest friend for help but all are in surprised mood, so in no condition to help, so cursing ourselves we wrote our exam.

After the exam all our mates said same thing, "Arey I didn't write well ra, I am going to fail ra."

Listening to this I felt happy, thank God some fellows are there with me, but after the results those bloody guys got good marks.

No, what and how, how did they get such marks?

Now this was more surprising for me, if I asked them then they said, "Arey I don't know ra, I don't know how I got also, thank you God, thank you." They cried like this, on seeing which my eyes turned red and really I scolded them very badly, and I scolded myself in my mind.

Whatever it may be it was a superb past.

In that year's quarterly exam, I got another superb experience. This incident happened after the exam.

"I got 81% confidence from this incidence."

Eighth class 2005, after the quarterly exams…

Our quarterly exams were completed and we got ten days Dussera holidays. Dussera holidays were also completed happily. And now it was time to get tension and time to get scolding.

School had started, in the first period we got one subject's answer sheet. My marks in that were just average. We got the answer sheet of another subject in the second period, and one after the other we were getting the answer sheets. Here we have to remember that my younger sister was also studying in the same school. After every unit test she would show her answer sheets and progress card, but as for me I would not. I didn't show any answer sheet because my mom's signature was so easy and my dad's also, so I didn't find it necessary for answer sheets, but for the progress card I needed their signature, so I would show the progress card.

After the Dussera holidays our teachers play with us. During the holidays they fight with our answer sheets by using red ink pen. After the holidays they produce our feedback. And now we have to fight with the answer sheets to get a parent's signature on it.

My sister is a top scorer so normally she shows all her answer sheets. Seeing her papers my dad gave an aggressive look at me, that's it and he didn't ask any questions about my papers, because he knows very well about me. But my mom was not like my dad. She asked about the papers but me, I'm a grown up kid, so I bluffed in reply. But she is my mom, I had grown up in front of her eyes, so she never accepts my answers, and she didn't ask any second question also. And she can't be silent.

In the holidays another danger landed on me from Guntur. It was my brother. He didn't get a medical seat so he had gone for a long term coaching in Guntur.

So for Dussera holidays he came home but after the holidays he didn't go back immediately, he spent two more days. My mom was asking about my papers but I was giving false answers which she didn't accept, and she told this to my brother. Then this "most sincere person of India" came and asked the same questions, and again I gave the same bluffing answers. He was not like my mom, he was my brother, and just two years back he completed his schooling, and he was also a cunning fellow, so how could he accept my answer? Nope, he didn't accept my answer. He started searching my bag.

"Here I made a mistake, I said a lie but I didn't make it true."

"To escape from a problem if you tell a lie, then make it true, if not you will be stuck like me."

My brother started searching; slowly he started getting my answer sheets, one after the other answer sheets were coming out from my bag. My marks were "not bad to not good," like above fifty-five and below sixty. So I was feeling a little tension but not that much. These were not fair marks but ok these were my marks. But the problem was biology, where I got 36 marks in that subject. I had just passed in that just by a single mark. If he found that paper then… my fear kicked me to hell. I was tense and he was searching; but biology was not found. He was searching even though he didn't know about my biology, but he was searching for some more papers. I decided that I was going to get caught, a little fear and a little tension, these were my lowest marks after I started studying. If he saw my biology paper nothing was going to happen, he won't scold me, he would just say, "You are going back."

In the seventh he said, "Arey you are getting good in studies ra, keep it up like this." So now if he says that you are back, no I didn't want those words. I had changed; I had started learning from seventh class. These thirty-six marks belongs to before seventh; now I'm a 60% student, so this thirty-six marks are not mine, it tensed me much. I was counting seconds. My pulse rate was getting low. Why did I get low marks? No, the problem is not me, my biology teacher gave me low marks. What would have happened if she had given good marks ha. Until now I scolded myself, and now I scolded her also, because of her I was standing in tension. In movies we find a character that has so many problems, and is waiting for a hero to save him from his problems. My situation was also like that character's. Waiting for a hero… At the dead end of the situation, I was saved.

Before I could get caught, luck arrived in the form of my brother's friend. In the nick of time he came and called my brother; my brother stopped checking and went out.

Heoooooo goddess!

I'm saved, I escaped.

God must be crazy, really God must be crazy, crazy.

Until that time, I was standing in attention position, tension in eyes, my sweat glands overflowing with sweat, little shivering in hands and oxygen was stuck in my nose, it wouldn't flow in and out. When his friend called him out, then I relaxed. That minute I found my luck. Before moving out he said, "Arey just once try to study, you can see the difference. If you don't see any change then leave your studies. Don't look back ra, only a few fellows are there behind you; see how many are in front of you," and he moved out. I don't know why, but in that minute those words directly reached my brain, I think because of fear and tension.

You know, luck stays by the side of ill luck. If we are stuck in a problem, when oxygen is stuck in the nose without any in and out flow, and our life is also going off..! At that minute luck enters and slaps us ooffff! We get relaxed, then we start breathing, and at that minute we feel the value of luck. The sound from the mouth "ooofff" is the expression of luck.

At that time, for me too luck entered in the name of my brother's friend. From here luck started entering into my life irregularly. More than luck, my brother's words moved deep into my brain. I don't know what would have happened if I didn't get lucky.

I started studying for the next unit test. I prepared well and this was the first time that I prepared whole heartedly. I studied like a topper. I had never ever prepared like this. It was the third unit test exam, and in that test I got 81% marks. 60% to 81% marks. This was my highest ever marks during my schooling. In the seventh public exam I got above 75% marks, but that was not all fair marks as 10% marks were earned by decoration of answer sheets, which means it was due to lose evaluation. This 81% was my own earned marks which were corrected by our teachers. These marks showed what I am and what I can do.

Until then during exam times I used to look around the class to get help, but in this test I never looked around, because I knew the questions and answers, and the funniest thing is that I helped so many rascals in the exam. From this I understood that a rascal can also help other rascals.

Actually I got help from those fellows but in this 3rd unit test I helped those who helped me in the previous exams. The feeling was awesome. After the exam some fellows said, "Arey today he helped me a lot ra, he showed two questions."

How cool it sounds!

God, so pleasant to listen to! Don't know every time how a clever enjoys this pleasant feeling. But for me really I enjoyed good.

When we are in tension or we are facing any fear, in that bloody time if we get any smooth words then we surrender to that words. "Our fear, our tension can make anything of us."

To learn something, first we have to know the value of something. Going near to hell and coming back with luck that was the chance I got.

Yes I feel the change and I see the change; I agree with my brother. If we study once we can see the change. I understand this from my brother. Life is a little interesting; not only my brother, I got this from my sister, from mom, from my brother's friend and from my marks. If I had got 60 marks in biology, then I would have missed my 81% capability. Because of my sister and my mom and my brother who checked my bag, and that he told me to try once. So due to all these reasons I found myself and my 81% capability. If I miss anything in the above then I also missed this 81%

"So behind every good cause a lot of hateful reasons are present."

And I conclude one more thing, studying is the easiest way, it is the easiest work than any other thing. For human beings there are only two easiest works, one is "studying" and other one is "thinking," but all the gutsy guys are far from these things. They do the hard work and they themselves conclude that it is too easy. They leave the easiest work and then they scold themselves after they lose. But I found it sooner. But even I didn't develop any interest in studies. My 81% also couldn't make me get interested in it.

It shows what I can, but not what I want.

My 81% made me proud, it spells what I can do, and it says study is not tough for me. I am not triggering, that's the problem I have. From then on I didn't cry for studies. It showed what I can but not what I want.

After the third unit test I never studied like that, because in eighth standard, apart from studies I learned enjoyment, I learned running and some more extracurricular activities also. All this extra stuff dominated my studies.

I had confidence, so if there is no use for studies, if I want to get good I can. So this thought makes me proud.

My extracurricular activity:

In this class I learned the meaning of "tonsured" and I saw a lot of changes in a week. Within seven days a lot can happen; I saw this in this class. In a week my total life turned 360+360 degree.

Here I found the meaning of INFATUATION.

I fell into a crush.

- Looks
- Like
- Crush
- Peaks of liking

- Style
- Making myself to beautiful
- Tonsured

First day: While going to tuition every time we had a good chit chat and in that we talked more about girls. While of chatting I heard a word "LOVE" hoo sounds are too tooo toooo good to hear. Hearing that my ears were tickled, from then I fell in love with the word love. Very interesting four letter words, it tempts me big.

One fine day I saw a beautiful girl, and I fell into a crush. It was my first crush. Awesome day, awesome crush on a cute and bubbly girl. Already hormonal changes had started. I started looking her. No alphabets are there to express my feelings and no numbers are there to rate my enthusiasm. She is a beauty, a beautiful girl. I congratulated my eyes every time because they got a chance to enjoy her beauty. She was so beautiful and her color was like my palm; I think her grandparent had a little connection with foreigners, so that's why she was that much fair. She was made with milk and sugar without sugar we can't drink milk. "So without her we can't derive the equation of beauty."

From that day onwards my eyes started seeing her. My eyes liked searching for her. She was not my school mate. She was my tuition mate. That was where I saw her and I developed a crush for her. Only looks on the first day. We don't know at what time we will meet our beautiful crush, and if we get that we also would like to turn beautiful to fall on her eyes, but we don't know the time. That's why only we fall in crushes with untidy faces but girls do not.

Falling in a crush is quite good and the feeling is a little romantic. "She was my first girl."

Second day: When I saw her for first time I was surprised by her beauty. What a beauty she was. I was infatuated with her beauty. From there I entered the second step of liking her more. My eyes liked her very much. So during tuition, there was no study, no interval, just watching her and enjoying her beauty. In my body lots of hormones were getting matured. Until now I had found only twelve colors like as in sketch pens, but now I am seeing 12,000 colors.

Hoo is it possible?

Yes it is possible Mr evoL.

If we are in crush anything can be possible with or without doubt. My spectacled eyes turn to beautiful and were finding everything beautiful, even my tuition teacher was looking chubby, and my tuition teacher's father, hoo God he was looking dam handsome yaar.

If anyone said she was beautiful, I smiled at them, but inside me my blood boiled.

I think

I fall in love yaar, I fall in love with beautiful.

I fell.

Third day: On the second day I liked her. I fell into infatuation with her. Now I moved to the next level. Now I am in love with her. Actually every human being can get dreams, but among us only 7 to 5 percent can remember our dreams after we get up. Now it turns to 0.0000001% more because I had entered. I fought with my brain to remember my dreams. On the third day no viral changes occurred, only a single change that is evoL. Crush turned to love.

Fourth day: Going to peaks in liking.

Four is not my lucky number but I liked four more than any other. On this 4th day lots had changed. After fighting with my dreams the interest on her moved to next level, now I was at peak stage. Now I was ready to die for her, I could do anything for her, anything with or without her permission. To gain her I could fight with anyone.

Now I was floating in dreams. Not only in night but in the school also I was in dramatic mood. I was not attentive in classes and was getting scolding also. In crush our matured hormones behaves senseless. Because of this we fall into problems.

Fifth day: The only work for me is to look at her and to enjoy her beauty. This is my work during the tuitions. I had been looking at her for the past four days, but she was not looking at me, so I decided to make her see, but I didn't have any plans to change her vision. But I had to do some stuff. After watching my friends I noted down some things. In that one was "Study;" hoo it's not a fair work because it's not under my control, I thought about the other plans. Then I found that one of my friends, had different hair style, it impressed me a bit, so changing my style is good and it was the best thing and I decided to change myself, and it was an easy way with no harm to me. But a special surprise was waiting for me.

Sixth day: After deciding to change my style, I went on the plan. I have to change my style from top to bottom. First I started from hair style. I was in dramatic mood, so my ideas were also dramatized. It was Saturday, and every Saturday we had a half day school. Afternoon was holiday for us, so on Saturdays we moved a little early to tuitions. So at 4 o' clock

I think, I went to the bathroom with a pair of scissor and mirror in hand. Actually I had hair cuts on Sundays, but I couldn't wait till the next day. And tomorrow was a holiday for tuitions, so if I had hair cut tomorrow, then I would have to wait till Monday, and I can't wait. My interest in her pushed me into the bathroom. Outside my mom was grinding wheat and my dad was reading news paper, sipping tea. After ten minutes I opened the bathroom door slowly I came out. On seeing me my mom was quite shocked and my dad was astonished, stunned, amazed etcetera. Even I was shocked by their reaction; I didn't except this from them, silently I went in and I looked at the mirror.

What the hell is this, now I understood why my parents reacted like that. In the bathroom I had trimmed my hair myself. My hair style looked like a disease called 'alopecia'. It looked vulgar.

God damn!

Shit, with this hair style.

With this style how can I go to tuition and how can I show my face to my crush

Hoo God what have you done?

My dramatized dream blurred me, I cried.

I wept.

Seeing my hair style my dad scolded me. And I didn't go on that day.

I cried a lot on seeing my face.

What had I thought, and what the hell had I done!

Seventh day: On the next day, it being Sunday, I went weeping to the saloon to clean up my style; I had worn a cap while going there. Even the saloon boy was surprised to see my hair style and he laughed.

"Who made your crop?" He asked.

"I only," I replied.

"What?" Again he was shocked.

After a while he started his work, he tried to make my trimmed hair clean and neat, and to give it a decent look, but he couldn't get a good crop. Although he tried a lot, he was not getting it and he didn't get a neat look. This shows how badly I had cut my hair.

At last he got an idea and said to me, "Kid, close your eyes, I will cut you a wonderful style." Those words made me feel good and I closed my eyes with pleasure.

He used the razor and tonsured my head on one side. I opened my eyes.

"Anna, what is this, what are you doing," I cried.

"Anna, what anna, what are you doing?"

"Brother this is the only way to make your hair look neat and good."

Yes it was the only hair style which was suited for me, and no other barber could do better than this, so tell me he questioned?

Already he had tonsured me on one side, so what could I say? With this half tonsured hair how could I move to another saloon? I couldn't. He had tied my hands.

"Ok anna, do as you like," I whispered. He cleared all my hair, clean, neat and good hair style.

"He tonsured me."

My first crush made me tonsured. My first love ended within a week.

My crush started on Monday and it turned worst on Saturday and it turned wild on Sunday.

When I was three years old my parents tonsured me at Thirupathi. After that I had never done it. My mom used to say every time, "Arey we want to go to Thirupathi ra."

But for the past few years we had not moved.

When my mom talked about Thirupathi, I always said no, because I didn't like the idea of giving all my hair to God.

But now I had surrendered all my hair in a saloon shop ……

I think lord Venkateswara had a grudge on me, so that's why he did this to me.

The next day I went to school. My friend asked about my tonsure, "Where were you tonsured ra, is it in Thirupathi? Then where is Thirupathi laddu ra," he asked.

"No ra not in Thirupathi, I had it done here only," I replied.

He laughed at me. I also laughed.

Who made me like this, my crush or my senseless thoughts, or lord Venakateswara?

"A harmonious senseless thought on my lovable crush made me like this."

When we are in crush we do a lot of extracurricular activities. When seeing a girl we decide that she is our angel, in the first two three days we love her, and then we try to impress her, we try to flirt with her, we try so many things to get her, and in this process we forget about loving her.

"But in love we don't do any extra activities, we just show our love for her. So that's why we call it as love, and we call that other one crush."

In the eighth standard I learned all sorts of nonsense, and in studies I got a new confidence that I am also good in my subjects.

From here my life started in all the activities.

My crush…

My 81% …

My tuition and my little nonsense…

Confidence…

Everything went up from here. Before this year I was a little dumb. From this year my coated nonsense started.

2006–2007

9TH CLASS

Eighth class made my time good. Here I forgot to mention a person who is my guide, my spiritual guide. He is the reason for my change, so I treat him as my spiritual guide. He is Mr. Vinod. He rides me out, he made me thief, and he kicked me out of my reserved nature. In the primary classes he was my enemy, but later in the higher sections he became my friend. No other words to describe him, other than that he is my 'FRIEND.'

In the ninth I moved a step ahead. An unforgettable incident happened when I was in this class.

In our school every standard had two sections, sections A and B. From LKG onwards I belonged to B section. I joined the B section in LKG, and until the eighth class we had two sections. After that, i.e., from the ninth onwards both the sections were joined and formed into one section. The reason was that from this time onwards, the teachers had to make us fight well in the 10th. So taking two sections was tough; making them into one section and giving the best time to study was good to beat the competition in the town.

So both our sections were combined and formed into a single section. I knew about A-section but I was not that much close to them. A-sections guys were intelligent fellows, good fellows and blah blah blah, I had heard these words from my teachers because every time our teachers praised A-section fellows. From now onwards we sat in the same class, so now I could see how good they were. New friends and new beautiful flowers arrived. But one thing is correct; they looked beautiful.

In that section I found two guys like me, they were Ashok and Dica. Dica's real name is Srikanth, but we call him Dica. Here I want to say something about Ashok. In the previous class he used to sit beside his sister in the girls' row due to scarcity of space. In the ninth, both sections were combined together, so here also the same adjustment problem had occurred. My class teacher suggested the same thing to Ashok, but this time he expressed regret and he said, "No ma'am I won't; in the eighth class I faced so many problems, so now I won't ma'am," he cried.

In the previous class he sat in the girls' row. In the eighth we had a teacher named Beulla, who took physics. She didn't ask any questions, she just gave them to the students in lists. She placed it like a contest. The contest was like this, boys ask question to girls, and girls asks to boys, but both boys and girls forgot this fellow, so no one asked even a single question to him. Sometimes teachers too did the same thing because he sat in the middle of the girls. This neglect made him feel very bad. Due to this incident, in the ninth he didn't accepted ma'am's suggestion. So, just for him ma'am brought another bench and adjusted the places.

In the ninth some of my classmates left the school. I felt a little bad, but later I adjusted, because in the ninth odd number of colors entered my life. A huge hormonal imbalance happened in the previous year, and now this many colors, how could I escape from this.

In the ninth I developed crushes for three girls. It was not a crush; I liked these three girls. All of them belonged to A-section.

1. First girl, I liked her name… She had a sweet name, I liked her name and she impressed me with her name.
2. Second girl, I liked her voice… She had a sweet voice, her voice was a little like that of a black cuckoo. While she spoke, it was so pleasant to listen. Even in hundreds of people, also I can find her voice easily because she has that much sweet voice.
3. Third girl, I liked her in total… Totally she looked beautiful; she walked like a goddess, and Goddamn happens in my brain while she was walking.

These three girls belonged to A-section. So they had some pride about themselves.

"One of these girls made me angry without my permission. After that she made me breathless."

One fine Wednesday I was beaten up by my teacher because of her.

Let's move into the story. One of my teachers conducted a slip test. All of us wrote the slip test in our assignment books. After the exam he didn't take the assignment books with him. He placed the books on my desk. I sat on the first bench in the first row. During the evening study hour I did some nonsense; not only me, but one of my classmates, also did nonsense. It was the study hour but all were nasty fellows in the class room, so all the guys were doing nonsense, and I was one of those guys. In a class room both dull and clever people are present, just like there are good guys and bad guys also present. So our class also had a mix of both categories.

I didn't know who were the good ones and the bad ones. From the previous year onwards I had started learning, and only then had I started sizing up the persons, so it took time to distinguish the good and the bad. So the next day, it was a Wednesday, duringhis period, sir entered the class room and he asked for the assignment books and started the correction. Then this 'sincere one of our school' and of our class, woke up from her place and said, "Sir yesterday in the evening study hour some guys rewrote in the assignment books sir."

She cried!

Hearing her words sir said ok, spelling out her name, he spelled ok. "!@#$%^&"

I had been hearing her name for the past few months, but now her name sounded very beautiful to hear. It sounded pretty good while sir was calling her name. My attention went to her.

"Who are those guys please get up," sir shouted

Yesterday during the study hour all had done nonsense, and I had also done some nonsense, but rewriting the answers in the assignment books, no, I didn't do that. Some of my fellows had done that and I just transferred the books, so I was not the accused here, I was just the witness for the nonsense. So I didn't take it serious and I was also looking eagerly for those guys. But a sudden surprise was waiting for me.

Sir again asked, "Who are those guys, please get up!"

No response from boys.

"Who are those guys @#$%^&" Sir asked her.

The first time I was a little surprised on hearing her name, the second time again I heard her name "!@#$%^&"

Why was I am feeling surprised? I knew her name but still on that day I felt a little surprised. What a cool name she has. I was seeing her and my attention was on her. For the first time after two to three months from the school reopening, I was looking at her for more than a few minutes. She wore the white uniform looking like a "fatty angel" and there was a fair amount of anger on her face because of those guys. I thought that if she were a teacher then what would be the situation of those guys. I laughed to myself.

Then she spelled out those guys' names.

What the heck?

She spelled my name too!

What?

Was I hearing my name or someone else's, what happened to my ears?

I didn't get it. What had I done yesterday, no I didn't do it.

Within a second, "fatty angel turned to fatty ghost."

Yes, yesterday I had done some nonsense on our bench with the assignment books, but it was not rewriting. But she thought I was the accused.

Sudden surprise for me....

I explained it to sir. But he was not listening; he was thinking that he was the only sincere teacher in the school. And he cited the cat and milk proverb.

He tore my skin.

I got angry with her. I decided to take revenge on her.

Students are nasty fellows; if we give a chance to them really they will do nonsense. Turning to nasty is not our fault, it is the teachers who are making us like this. He didn't take the assignment books with him, he kept the books on our desk, and that was his fault. And he quoted the story. Cat drinks the milk closing her eyes and thinks that no one is seeing

Cat is cunning, searching for milk is her habit. Placing milk near the cat is our mistake. So before beating the students first we have to check. Saying proverb, and thinking that we are super is not fair.

I got angry with my sir also.

But it was ok for me; because of this incident I got her. But even I decided to take revenge.

The next day in the class room, I saw her with anger, and I decided to take revenge on her, but the emotion is not in my control, hoo God! Again she was looking like a fatty angel.

No ra, she is not an angel she is the devil, I explained to myself, but my feelings could not be controlled. She was becoming my second crush.

No, I didn't want it, already I had experienced the crush, it is worse than ever.

"No God no, I don't want it," I wept.

I decided to stop thinking about revenge on her. No revenge, nothing, and I tried to ignore her. But I couldn't because,

"We can't escape from angels and devils." However much we hesitate, even then we run after them. It's our weakness.

"We can escape from laughter but not from happiness."

"We can escape from crying but not from sadness."

"We move far from emotions but not from feeling."

"So we escape from everyone, but not from devils and angels."

And we can't escape from love.

Again I fall in crush. But it was not like my earlier crush.

And about her looks, really she was a "fatty angel". She looked like a boiled egg.

I didn't do any special actions because I had experienced that in my first crush. So I decided not to do any extracurricular activities this time.

Previous one was just infatuation at that time I thought it was love but within week I understood.

Without any mistake on my part, fatty made me angry, and without her permission I started liking her.

My second crush makes me breathless. She was not beautiful, she was a fatty beauty and she was a little cute also. And now I had no anger with her. I liked her, I liked her a lot.

In school times I just enjoyed her fatty looks.

I did not improve in studies in the ninth. I moved with 50 to 60 percent only. But I improved in nonsense, although until now no teacher caught me.

I was not a good kid… But still no one caught me.

In the quarterly exams, due to malpractice, one of my teachers tore my physics bit paper. After the exam my physics teacher gave out our answer sheets and he showed his action on the students who didn't get good marks. I was also in the list because Babu Sir tore my bit paper and he attached another blank bit paper, so I got zero marks in bit paper.

On that day I was absent so I escaped. Next day my friends told me about the situation and his actions on the previous day. I was in tension and I was frightened also. During the physics period sir called out the absentees. He looked at me and asked why I didn't attempt the bit paper.

"Sir, I answered bit paper, sir but invigilator misunderstood me and he thought that I had copied so he tore my bit paper sir," I replied.

"Seeing you I'm not getting angry with you ra," he said.

My innocent face and innocent words saved me. From my childhood onwards no one got angry with me and no one noticed my nonsense, even my friends didn't know my nonsense, they thought I'm a good kid.

Here I had done a malpractice in the bit paper that's why invigilator tore my paper.

In ninth, during the exam time, some fellows were caught having slips and in every class our sports sir was searching for those guys. I was also in that but I escaped. I had a slip in my pocket. If I had been caught all the fellows would have treated me same as the others. But I was saved.

Because of my innocent looks I escaped. From then on I decided not to take any slips. If I had a chance I took help from my mates, but slips no, I decided strongly. Because if I caught all will treat me like as others. So I said no to slips.

I'm a nonsense good kid.

In ninth my rewriting moved a step ahead. Class to class my nonsense also promoted. After the quarterly and half yearly exams we get ten days holidays in the name of the Dussera festival and Christmas. And in the holidays our intellectual nonsense starts. Some of our teachers took our answer sheets home and some of them corrected our papers during the examination time itself, and kept the corrected papers in the staff room. So during the holidays we made a plan to rewrite our marks. So we went to school in the guise of playing, but our actual plan was to rewrite our papers. We played in the school till the watchman left, and after he went off then our cunning nonsense started.

We went to the backside of the staff room and we started our plan. Getting in through the staff room window, we took hold of the corrected papers and corrected the questions and answers as we liked, and in uncorrected papers we added extra additional sheets and we replaced them in the same place.

After the holidays a miracle happened in the result.

We got our expected marks in some papers, but in some papers we didn't.

Sometimes if I was dissatisfied with the marks, after getting the progress card I did some modifications in the card…All because of too much hankering after marks.

Because of this excessive hankering I met with a problem, a big problem.

Every day is not our day. Sometimes it becomes someone else's.

After all the nonsense I showed my card to my dad. On seeing the card my dad asked some questions.

The first question he asked was, "Is this your marks?"

There's no need to be surprised, because my card looked like a rubbed copy writing book; I had rubbed on my original marks and rewritten over them, so obviously some questions would arise.

Strongly and boldly I replied. "Dad it is not an answer sheet to rewrite, it is the progress card, how is it possible dad, and how has my class teacher accepted it," I replied strongly.

Hearing my bold and confident words, he put his signature without raising any second question.

In the eighth class I learned how to convert a lie into truth. So easily dad put his sign.

Yes, my dad had asked a correct question. If my class teacher saw this what could I do, what explanation could I give? While rewriting in card I didn't think about my class teacher, I thought only about today so now I was stuck in problem.

I started thinking about the next day.

Actually my class leader collected the progress cards; he just checked whether the parent's signature was there or not, that's it, he didn't check the card. If he had done so, I was ready with an answer, what I had said to my dad, so there was no need to worry. After collecting the cards my class teacher would also check the signatures, and if she noticed any untidiness in the card she would call me and ask, and if she didn't get a good answer then she would verify the marks from the mark list book if there is any change in the card. Then I would be caught.

So I decided not to give the card, I didn't submit my card; not only I, some of my friends also did not submitted. Due to their own problems they didn't submit.

The class leader submitted the collected cards. Here my class teacher made a mistake that she didn't count the cards and she didn't count the remaining candidates. Ma'am left the class and I was safe.

Next day some of my fellows submitted their cards and some did not. Now ma'am took the names. Here my friend and I didn't give our names, so we both escaped. Now ma'am left out with our names.

Day by day one by one submitted their cards but I did not.

After three days all had submitted their cards, and now ma'am took the count, and my card was missing. Ma'am called out my name, and asked, "Your card is missing, have you submitted your card?"

"Yes ma'am, I submitted," I replied.

"I checked for it in the staff room also, it's not there, really have you submitted it or not?"

I was standing in the middle of the class.

The whole class was silent.

I could hear my own breathing.

"Yes ma'am, I submitted," I replied.

"Then where is your card? It's not here," now she shouted.

In a moaning voice, "Yes ma'am, I submitted on the first day itself," I cried.

Ma'am was losing her patience.

I don't know what to say, my cerebrum started its work to get an answer and my nerves were aroused, but I was not getting a proper reply. I decided that I was going to get caught. Here again I was stuck in a problem.

I didn't know what to say, either truth or falsehood.

I was trying to make it true.

Ma'am became serious.

Again and again ma'am was asking and she was receiving the same answer from my side.

The entire class was watching me.

I'm decided I'm going to be caught. From now all in the class think that I'm also a nonsense kid. This was my last minute. After this minute I'm also taking place in between nasty fellows.

Lastly ma'am asked to the class whether anybody had seen me giving the progress card.

I decided that I was caught because no one in the class had seen me giving the card, because it was in my bag and I hadn't submitted the card, so how could anyone in the class see it.

But I escaped.

Here my luck slapped me from the back bench.

My friend Vedavyas, he stood up and said, "Yes ma'am I saw while he was giving."

God!

I was shocked.

My card was in my bag, but he was saying that he had seen me giving it.

How?

How did he say that he had seen me submitting it?

It was quite mysterious.

For the past ten minutes I had been saying that I had submitted the card, but ma'am had a little doubt in her, but she was not blaming me, actually no one could blame me because of my innocent looks. But she didn't try to check my bag.

And she asked the class whether anybody had seen it or not, and then Vedavyas stood up and said that he had. Again I was saved.

A lie with an innocent face can make anything true.

And a friend with innocent trust in me, made my lie a truth.

A lie, a blind lie.

Really luck must be crazy. And God he is too crazy.

Make the lie big, make it simple,

Keep saying it, and eventually

They will believe it.

....Adolf Hitler

"Making a lie is an art, make it more beautiful, and even tremendous truth also can't stand before the traditional lie."

At last ma'am believed me and I got another card.

After the exams we went on tour. It was my first tour. We went on a tour of two days in the cold season. I enjoyed a lot. It was my best first tour experience.

In the ninth I found the value of friends and the value of robbery.

In the eighth I learned about stealing things from gift shops. I learned this from Vinod, he was good at that. While going to tuition we used to do this nonsense. We moved into fancy stores and we stole greeting cards, chocolate boxes, etc. My whole gang was good at this except me, so I was impressed by them. So I also learned by observing them. The first time I stole a greeting card I succeeded.

Ooohoooo. What a feeling it was. When I got 81% marks I felt happy; it was not a happy, but a good feeling.

81% showed my capability. I can't forget the feeling I had on that day in front of my father, and the same feeling I found again on stealing the greeting card. I behaved in same way before my friends. Really stealing things from shops is a pleasurable experience. I enjoyed steeling.

But stealing from shops is totally different when compared with stealing from home. If mom was not at home, we used to steal coins, but in the shop we have to steal things in the presence of the shop keeper. It is an amazing and exciting experience. And most exciting job. After experiencing it, I felt respect for thieves. What a creative intellectual job it is.

I won and I felt proud also. Easily I learned to steal, my happiness touched the sky. After stealing my friends used to feel very proud, and I too felt like them. At home although I was very proud, I kept it in concealment.

After many days I tried a second time, but this time a surprise was waiting for me. I was caught by the shopkeeper.

Ooohoooo.

This time I failed.

In life we get so many surprises but this type of surprise we never expect; when I stole the first time I felt very proud, and now this time I stood in front of the shop keeper in shame. Gaining and losing in the same place.

Shameful experience, I lost myself, standing before someone like a thief is the worst and most painful experience.

Yesterday I won and today at the same place I lost.

I had done this for fun, but sometimes fun is the most dangerous thing; I understood this after its turning to the worst experience.

I learned stealing by observing them, but I didn't learn how to escape.

In this situation I notice one thing, making mistakes in the same place and same pattern is the first step to failure. So don't make mistakes in the same way. Try to change, make it different and make it big. If not you will be caught like me. I made the same mistake and I got caught.

And the most important thing while doing nonsense is, don't do it singly. Do it on behalf of friends or do it with your friends. When I was caught by the shop keeper I was frightened, and didn't get how to escape, but here I was not single. My fellows were also with me. All of us had intended to steal things, but before that I was caught by the shop keeper. I escaped the shop keeper's anger because of my friends. My friends made him cool.

'Raghavendra'

Without him nothing happens. Without him I can't imagine how the situation would have been. With him we could do so many nonsensical things, malpractices, robbery, etc.

He was my class mate and he was the gang leader for nonsense. He was good at talking; he was just like 'water' which can mold into any shape like solid, liquid and gas. He made the shop keeper cool down; not only he, another mate Srikanth also cooled down the shop keeper. This was the second time this fellow Srikanth had helped me. He was the one who had encouraged me to steal greeting cards, but after I got caught he preached me morals. Hoo God more than getting caught, it was so painful for me; he killed me with his morals.

I don't know what they said but they saved me. I escaped, and after the incident we moved to the tuition. All my friends started teaching how to escape and they started spelling out morals.

Shit!

All my idiots turned to good fellows, and now they were teaching me morals.

Ok.

It was my turn to listen to morals.

My first robbery was good but my second was not. I experienced both with a same incident.

Two things I learned.

1. Don't make mistakes in the same way, try to make some change.
2. Do mistakes on behalf of friends. It helps you to escape.

If you are interested in stealing then do it and don't do it by impression.

In another incident because of this Srikanth I got caught by the shop keeper. We both went to a shop to buy a book but he returned without giving money, and the sales boy caught me and the shop keeper took the money from me.

However in the school maybe we ruled our schooling and we enjoyed our days.

Ninth is good year for me.

Beautiful year, I enjoyed lot in this year.

Here I found everything in real.

I found real meaning of crush

I found real meaning of friends

I found real enjoyment

I learned lying.

2007–2008

10TH CLASS

In 9th final exams I got 500 marks which were not mine this was only my progress card marks. On seeing the marks my dad increased his hopes on me and decided that I was going to be the top scorer in our family.

Now I entered 10th class. This is the last standard of schooling and most important standard for all things.

10th is not like 7th. Easily I got good marks in 7th but it is not possible in 10th If I made any extras then 10th would kick me out. So I decided to make some space for studies.

My 10th started with tension, up to 7th I was a below average kid, but after that I had become a 60% kid. Not only in studies, my enjoyment also had moved to 60%.

In 7th standard correction is easy, but in 10th the correction was little scary. So in under condition I decided to beat the record.

Here my "fatty kid" also entered the 10th standard. I had been seeing her all these days, but I did not bother to impress her. Mine was a one sided crush.

From 9th onwards our class was fully loaded with crushes. Untidy faces turned to neat and tidy hair style.

"A huge hormonal imbalance..." The entire class was filled with crushes.

"Day by day, one by one, idiot by idiot was falling into crush."

Falling in crush was like dancing in front of an angry bull wearing red dress. We knew the risk but still we fell into that; in the 8th I had experienced it, but within a year again I fell into crush, and now that I was in the 10th it was still on.

Why do these girls look so beautiful? And why do we fall in love? Even Shah Jahan can't give an answer to this.

On Saturdays every idiot looked neat and tidy. On Saturdays we wore civil dress to school, not uniform. This was the only day we had to show up in our tidy looks. Everyone came to school in tidy looks.

Some fellows were already in crush, so they wanted to show off their most impressive looks.

Some fellows were not in crushes, but still they came looking tidy. They didn't know whom to impress, but they wanted to impress someone and wanted to fall in someone's eyes?

Some fellows were in crush, but they were at a dumb level, they didn't want to try to impress, they just enjoyed their crushed feeling. They also come in tidy looks.

I was also one of the members in the above category.

Some courageous fellows explored their emotions on Saturdays and some did not. I too enjoyed Saturdays. My ninth standard ran successfully like a silent movie and my tenth also started progressing in the same way as the ninth.

Whatever was going on in our thoughts, our teachers disturbed it with studies.

Our teachers spoke all the time about the studies, about the correction. They guided us how to prepare, how to write, and how the correction will be done.

Nonsensical thoughts were running in my mind, and with this feeling I decided to study. No expectations, no restrictions… I felt free in mind. Even my dad formed a good opinion about me because after 7th I turned to 60%; so he believed me, and after 9th final exam he concluded that I was also going to be a topper in my family, so he didn't say anything.

My study days were going well. At that good time a problem arose. I don't know how to describe it, whether it was a problem or not. From here onwards problems started knocking at my door.

One fine afternoon my sister and I came home for lunch. Actually from my childhood up to the 10th, I used to come home for lunch. Our school was just five minutes away from home, so not only I, my brother and my younger sister too, all of us came home for lunch.

Like any normal routine afternoon we came home, but that afternoon my mom hadn't made any food. When we went for lunch my mom and dad were sitting opposite to each other. I didn't understand anything, why both of them were silent. My brain worked fast and tried to assess the situation. I thought that they had got into a fight. I moved to mom's side, and asked what happened and why both of them were silent. Then in a moaning voice mom replied, "Your dad is retiring next month."

What?

My sister was not grown up enough to think about it, but I was a little grown up. I knew what retiring meant and what happens after retiring. Until now we had thought that he had two more years for retirement, but before that my dad was retiring. My dad was retiring before completion of my schooling. My mom was feeling very bad that no one was settled, that all were still studying. My elder sister was doing M Phil, my brother was doing medicine 2nd year, I was in the tenth, and my younger sister was in 6th. From now earnings were going to be low, and no heavy expenditures could be made. I just didn't know what to think. I was not getting the answers to any questions.

After retirement my dad would get pension, but with a lower income. With this incident I made up my mind strongly that I wanted to study.

Covering our syllabus for the year also came to an end fast. From now onwards there would be only study hours, long study hours. I hated studying for a long time, I couldn't tolerate more than one hour of study. It was my weakness. So when I got bored while studying, I would try to motivate myself. In every class a topper will be present whose intention is only studying, studying and studying. We also had a topper. If I got bored I just looked at him and I got recharged and I found the energy to study. This was the self-motivation I got from outside.

I don't know how many fellows are interested in studies, but for a fellow who was not interested in studies, it was too horrible to study. If a student didn't get good marks in the 10th it was the worst thing ever. In our times getting good marks in the 10th was easy. If I didn't get it in 10th everyone would spits their emotions on my face. So I decided to study. However it may be, I had to study. So for this cause I tried to motivate myself anyway. The only aim was that I had to get 81% marks; I had to repeat my 8th class marks. I had to show "my potential."

"It was possible."

In 10th we again went on a tour, a long four days' tour.

"4 days of enjoyment."

And my b'day came up while we were on the tour.

I was not interested in b'day from my childhood. A tiny incident when I was in school… I celebrated my b'day, I don't remember which b'day it was; I went to school taking chocolates with me.

B'day's are very special to kids. We wear new dress, sweets, chocolates and all the stuff we need we will get on the special day not only in home even in school also we get special treatment if we do any nonsense on the b'day we didn't get any scolding from teacher. On the whole day all eyes are at us. So I like b'day's very much. Once I get results on my day but by seeing my result my dad didn't beaten, I surprised. So I like b'day's very very much. So with all excitement I went to school. So with over enthusiasm I distributed chocolates to my friends. But my class teacher scolded me badly because I didn't distribute chocolates, I just threw chocolates on my friends. With over excitement I behaved like that. That was the last time, and after that I didn't give any chocolates to any one and I didn't celebrate my b'day. From then I never went to school on my b'day's.

I enjoyed the tour a little, not too much and not so well.

On returning from tour the only work remaining was to study.

I started fighting with my books.

I had never studied like that ever before. I didn't even go to school on some days, I just stayed at home and I studied till a portion was completed. I put in leave for nearly fifteen days, and in that period, I studied only social studies. I don't know why I preferred social studies. But at last I completed it.

In the tenth standard social studies plays a key role in malpractice. Not only for me, but also for the whole class. Due to scarcity of teachers our head mistress had appointed a guest teacher for social studies. He was a skilled teacher; he worked in the government school. He was very good at social studies. In the evening hours, after completing his work at his own school, he came at 6 o'clock to our school to teach us. His teaching was excellent, and his decades of teaching experience made us good listeners.

"We are good listeners but not good rankers."

In the tenth also we did some malpractices, but we did the highest percentage of malpractice in social studies. After the exams sir gave us the answer sheets without marking any marks on it. He just gave us the corrected papers without entering any total on it, and said, "Add up your total marks and make a clear count by yourself and make sure whether any correction is required or not."

It looked like 'placing a dog to secure the hen,' and now we fellows showed our intellectual skills in malpractice. There was no difference between clever ones and duller ones. All fellows needed marks; some fellows needed ranks, so a single mark made him a ranker, and some fellows needed percentage, some fellows needed pass marks. Whatever the reason, for any problem a solution was there in the name of social studies. Everyone from ranker to dullard, all had a personal red ink pen for this subject.

From the sixth standard onwards we started using pens of two colors, one a red ink pen and the other blue. We wrote only questions with the red ink pen, and we wrote answers with blue ink pen on the note book. But after the exams this red ink was used to correct our marks also, so everyone had one red ink pen in their compass box. It meant that everyone had their marks in their own hands, and so everyone could rewrite their own fate. After getting the social studies papers we started changing our own fate, we rewrote our marks as per our wishes. Even a below average candidate got good marks in social studies. Not only the duller ones but even the cleaver ones also changed their fate, in total all changed their fate. In social studies all were equal. Some of the girls also did this. But this sincere of India never made a complaint on girls. I thought that she was favorable to girls and more so to A-section.

If there was a chance, there was no difference between clever and dull ones; all showed their capabilities in extracurricular activities.

The major interesting part in the whole scene was our social studies teacher. He didn't try to check the papers, and even if in some bad moments we were caught, he didn't even scold us. He was a good teacher.

Our class teacher went into shock while giving out the progress cards on seeing our marks. Sometimes our head mistress also perused the progress cards at random to check our marks, because we were in the tenth standard, and she wanted to check how we were doing. While going through the cards the HM also got a shock because all of us had got good scores in social studies. Some of the fellows who failed in one or two subjects had also got good marks, and seeing this, our head mistress was surprised at our marks. No one could understand the secret. I think they thought that our social studies teacher was the reason for all this. Yes he is responsible for all of us because his blind trust on us makes us like this. And we found so much enjoyment in the social studies period, not just because of the marks.

In this standard my HM beat me twice because of marks. She beat me in front of the whole class, and moreover in front of my crush, all because of the cursed marks.

In the tenth standard I faced another problem, but I didn't take it seriously. There was a parents meeting. I don't know why teachers hold parents meeting. During such meetings even teachers get their portion of scolding from parents. Even then they hold these meetings. Parents meeting means, teachers don't know our activities at home, and parents don't know our activities in school, so they sit together and discuss our activities in front of us.

After the half yearly exams our head mistress conducted the parents meeting.

During the half yearly exams so many nonsensical things happened like copying. Some of the fellows were caught by the invigilators, and we were drawing close to the public examinations. So our teaching staff decided to arrange a parents meeting as per the instructions of the head mistress. And another thing they decided was that they wanted to submit our progress cards in front of the parents, which meant that they wanted to hand over the cards to the parents. Knowing all this all the fellows like me started worrying. It was a sure thing, and there was no chance to escape.

On the day of the meeting, all the parents came to school to know about their children's performance. My mom and I went to school to collect the progress card. For the first time in my entire schooling I attended a parents meeting. The meeting was held in the office room. One after the other parents along with their children were going to the office room and getting the card. Some parents were happy with the result, and some were not. Some were happy with the results, but not with the behavior of their children. Some parents knew about their children, so they didn't take it too seriously and had come just for the sake of formality. Our teachers were revealing our nonsense.

My mom and I were waiting outside to be called, mom was feeling tense because she didn't know about me, which means she didn't know how I was in school and moreover she knew about my nonsense at home, I was the most worst kid at home but in school I was a good kid because I never caught by teachers. My mom didn't know this. So she felt some tension and mom was not ready to hear anything negative about me in front of others.

Seeing others, mom asked me, "Arey did you do any nonsense?"

"No ma," I replied.

But mom was not ready to trust me. Because…

When I was in the 5th class I had done nonsense. In the fifth class I got the 20th rank, which was the best rank for me up to the 7th standard. But I was not satisfied with that. I went home with a plan. I said, "Dad actually I got 19th rank but one of my friends also got the same total so my class teacher gave 19th rank to him and 20th rank to me."

I explained this to my dad.

Hearing this, my dad shouted, "How has he done like this? If both students get the same total he has to mention the same rank; how has he done like this ha!"

My dad shouted at me and he said to mom, "Hey Lakshmi go and ask him tomorrow."

Shit of my mouth, this was the first nonsense I had done without thinking, because I had got better rank when compared to previous unit tests, but why I did I make this explanation.

The next day mom came to school and asked my class teacher and he called me and asked, "What sir what have I done, and what have you said to your parents?"

I was surprised at that question.

I murmured, "Sir, sir…"

I murmured four times.

He understood my situation and sent me back to the class, and I don't know what he said to my mom. I was afraid, but mom didn't say anything to dad and didn't warn me also. Even my sir also didn't scold me and he didn't ask anything either. Some of the teachers understand better than parents.

This is what I meant, that mom was not ready to trust me. When I said no mom I didn't do any nonsense, she just nodded her head.

After a while the peon called me, it sounds like a fearsome call.

I and mom entered the office room; it was looking like a court. My head mistress was the prosecutor and my teachers were the witnesses for my mistakes, and I was the accused standing beside mom. Here the judge is my mom she has to hear the arguments and she has to give punishment.

They produced progress card and my HM asked the class teacher, “How is he in the class room?”

My class teacher said, “Ha ok ma’am but he is a little talkative.”

And my HM asked the remaining teachers.

One of my sirs said that, he is ok with studies but he as to improve to score well in public exams. That’s it.

My case was completed. They just warned me and sent me out.

My mom was happy that she didn’t get any complaints about me.

In the previous exams some of the fellows were caught copying, but I was not. In my entire schooling I was never caught copying, and I didn’t get any scolding even if I was caught. I’m a good fellow in nonsense.

Even after getting the card I rewrote on it. Seeing this, my brother asked, “I said arey its not answer sheet to rewrite the marks, it is ‘progress card’ ok?”

And no other question from my brother.

Like this our nonsense came to an end, and now it was time to study, only study.

Our teachers started giving us some guidelines about the exams, how to attempt and how to write and what are the requirements a student needs while writing exams. The first important guideline was hand writing and the second one is decoration. Decorating a paper gives the first impression for evaluation. Scrutinizers don’t know about our stuff so we want to impress them by decorating our answer papers. These guidelines we got from teachers. I got these guidelines in the 7th class also. No change, same guidelines.

Nothing has changed yaar, teachers have not changed, their guidelines have not changed, correction has not changed and we, how can we change, but the fear of exams has changed.

We got hall tickets. Within the week our exams were going to start. And now my tension increased, I had to make it in the exams, and I had set a huge target. I didn't know whether I would make it or not, but I had to do it.

Our public exams started.

Vinod and I were in the same center. With tension my first exam was completed, then the second exam and the third. In twelve days my exams were completed.

And during exams I met a girl, her name was Rani and she was from the government school. I still remember her. I don't know what her intention was towards me, but if she got answers from others immediately she shared with me, and she helped me very much in the exams. Other than that also she was a nice girl friend for me, and I enjoyed her company those twelve days.

I had written the exams well and my expected marks were 83.3333%.

Goddess, there is restriction for everything but for a wish there is no restriction. We can wish for anything.

But surprises are a regular friend for me, so something was waiting for me.

Actually I didn't study I just learned the subjects by heart, so as not to get surprises in the results.

When I got bored I looked at my class topper to get some recharge. I think that is a method of self-motivation, yes it is self-motivation, but I used it to learn the subjects by heart.

"Only wishes are mine, but not the things to make them real."

Hooooooooooo;

I forget the important thing,

It was my farewell party.

It was too important for me because from a few couple of emotions I had been waiting for this event. I was waiting for a chance to talk with her and to get her autograph, not only her autograph, I expected more; I expect her mobile number also. All boys and girls were wandering with slam books. I was also wandering looking for her to get her signature on my slam book; it was the last day for us. I had tried for a bit more, but I didn't have enough courage to talk. But I wanted her words, her autograph and her wishes. I was anguished for her signature. Some of my fellows were getting girls' autographs, and one fellow came and said except one I got all the girls' autographs on my slam. Hearing this I just just...... I was in anguish.

I was missing the time to get a talk with her, the sun had also left the sky and time was ticking off. God give me the courage to step ahead. I praised to god.

One of my friends was collecting the slam books and giving it to girls, and one by one the girls were putting their signatures on the slam books. Due to my diffidence I thought this should be the correct way to get her signature. I also gave him my slam book.

After ten minutes I got my slam book. I took it into my hands and eagerly I searched for her name with extra emotion, anxiously I turned the pages one by one fast, and the sounds that came from turning the papers while rotating them fast, even now I can hear those curious sounds.

Yes!

Hoo oo hoo I… I… I found it, I found her signature, she had signed at the ninth page of my slam book,

"Fatty angel."

I got you on my slam book you "fatty angel" I got you "fatty" I got you.

But a slight grief is that I got her autograph but didn't get her mobile number.

Ok fine, hoo I got her signature, I got her signature, I got her sign, I couldn't control my feelings. Any how I got you on my slam.

Yahoo hurray!

And a GIANT gaiety, from past two years this was the only emotional feeling that I could get from her. Physically and mentally I was attached with her.

"Physical feeling is, because of her I got beatings from sir."

"Mental feeling is by this incident some changes had occurred in my brain."

And I got beautiful words from her saying,

"'***You are thick because; I am close.***'"

These words I got from my crush…. It took six years for me to get the meaning.

The thing I didn't get till now is "fatty."

(She saw so many nonsenses but I didn't see her making complaints on others, she was good, but on that day why did she give a complaint on me, and what was I to think about that situation. I was not getting anything but by this incident I got her. And don't know in future what I would get from her.)

"*We learn loving from mom*

We learn handling problems and responsibilities from dad.

That's why we fall in love with girls

And making friends and fighting with boys."

But why this girl,

Why am I so crazy about her,

It was just an incidence, but it turned my emotion, I wandered for her. In the 8th I didn't get this much emotion; after tonsuring I forgot my crush, but in this case it has gone strong for two years.

Why?

Does she have any answer to this.

I didn't get why it happened, some incidents happen in our life, but by such happening some get something and some lose something.

I don't know what I got and what I'm going to lost.

For me also a day will come to ask my doubts to her.

Really God must be crazy.

He does all the naughty things and later he plays with us.

On farewell day I got so many good wishes,

Be in right way,

Move in straight,

And some do's,

And some don'ts.

And we guys discussed about higher studies, which branch and where we are joining. And we discussed about the exams that how to make our desired marks come true. We spelled our feelings till late evening and our farewell party came to end.

This was the last day in school. Twelve years ago, my mom dropped me in school with my pocket full of chocolates to stop me from crying. Now after twelve years I was going out from school with pocket full of enjoyment and with a handful of emotions and with tears in my eyes.

What we get from school is 'enjoyment' and what we lose after the school is also 'enjoyment.'

"A past life is real."

Malpractices, nonsense, crushes, friends, this all are symbols for schooling.

NONSENSE: This comes from attitude; we do nonsense of an innocent nature at kinder garden stage. But school makes every innocent a little too naughty, every good fellow turns a little nasty. If he does not, then he must be the worst student of the times. I'm a good fellow, no one knows about my nonsense. Good fellows mean they do nonsense on behalf of themselves, by luck and in a little intellectual way. These fellows escape from hell. Bad fellows mean they do on behalf of others and they are caught by teachers, that's why they are treated as bad fellows. But when we calculate in terms of the nonsense, both are the same. School turns every innocent fellow into good or bad, but it never changes an innocent fellow into too innocent; school gives a chance to every innocent kid to kick out his innocence. If we take that chance then we are the luckiest persons, and if we do not we are the most unlucky fellows because the age of ours never comes back. And the past never changes its footing.

MALPRACTICE: This we learn only during schooling. Without malpractice no exam will take place. It's our first right, yes malpractice is our first right. A teacher can't teach without a text book and a student cannot write an exam without copying, if there is no copying then there is no value for exam, if there is no copying there is no value for invigilation and no value for marks and no value for ranks. Because of us there is value for exams. So it's our first right. By doing malpractices we are giving good value for exams but if we get caught while copying then the teachers tear our skin ....

CRUSHES: Nonsense is a little noisy thing, malpractice is a little intellectual thing and crush is a little romantic thing. In schooling every fellow will experience this feeling. Crush means it is an emotional feeling for a person whom you like, but in schooling it is quite bitter, it means it is a feeling to show off ourselves to the person who looks beautiful. We try to impress her, don't know whether she likes us or not, and don't know whether we like her or not, but we wander for her, when she looks at us or if she talks to us in the class room, we just made rock and roll on the benches. On the farewell day one of my friends came to me and said, "Arey I get all girls' autographs except one." When he said that I was just a little startled. Why? He didn't say that he got good results or that he didn't win a cup, he just said about the girls. My expression has changed because he said 'girls'. Because they are the most curious and interesting parts for boys, no idiot can escape from them. No fellow can escape from crush. For one whole hour the teacher stands in front of us and teaches lessons, but we don't bother about it, but while a friend discusses someone's crush all the fellows surround us like ants surrounding sugar. And they listen to the discussion with much greater curiosity than they have for subjects. More than the subjects, girls and crush are the very important subjects for us. Falling in crush is an inexpressible emotion.

Hormonal changes: it occurs majorly during schooling. It doesn't matter how she looks, whether she is good or bad, is she beautiful or not – when it occurs everything turns to beautiful, every thin object turns fatty. I fell in crush during eighth class, but within a week my first crush crushed me. In ninth again I fell in crush but now it was an emotional feeling. She was not fair, and she was a little fat and she was not too tall, but I liked her. It was enough for me to fall into an emotional feeling. I liked her, I just liked her. If we have a friend from our school years, after that age he turns out to be a best friend, but if we have a crush in school she never turns to anything in life. Everyone says that it is infatuation or we gave some other name which occurs due to hormonal imbalance. But no one accepts that it is also an emotion; everyone stops by saying it is infatuation and there is no step forward for this emotion.

"Friendship is an emotional feeling, and like that crush in school days is also an emotional feeling."

"We accept friendship, but we don't accept a crush, and we name it as infatuation."

"Every crush is not an infatuation and every infatuation is not a crush."

FRIENDS: Nothing to say about these guys, the most annoying fellows, the worst fellows, they never teach us any lesson, they are just with us and push us forward, they never make us cry but they disturb us all the time, even in sadness also. We need a friend to scold us, we need a friend to tease us, we need a friend to makes us happy, we need a friend to show our anger on, we need a friend to escape, we need a friend to embarrass, we need a friend to laugh with, we need a friend to share, we need a friend to run, we need a friend to do nonsense, to lead all experiences. Just make a friend, I don't know what we get if we make a friend, but one thing is sure, we never lose anything by making friends, gain a friend to get a kick in life.

"What we get from school is enjoyment and what we lose from it is also enjoyment."

Nick name

Nick names… They have a special importance. No idiot can escape from nick names. Whatever name you may keep, there will always be a fellow to call you with nick name.

In LKG my long big name turned to short. And after that it underwent so many changes because of my friends. Names are sub-divided into two types and in that the first one is pet name. I have pet names which are used by my parents and relatives. They alone call me by those names. And another type of name is 'nick name'.

Every fellow who has friends normally has nick names. I also have so many nick names, of which one name that occupies the first place is "Discut." I got this name from my social studies teacher. While he called out my name it came out of his mouth as 'Discut.' Actually he spelled my name as 'Diskat', but my friends made it 'Discut.' This is my nick name, and now I turned to Discut. Some of my friends call me as Discut even now. It's a funny nick name. Our parents give us names by seeing zodiac signs and by counting stars, and by the date of birth. But without following any such tradition, our friends give us names. We call these nick names. Actually they remember our nick names more than the original names.

If you don't have any nick names,

It means you are not chilling with friends.

Anything you gain without this is worthless,

After parents only friends have a right to give us a name,

If you don't have any friends to name you and to call you by nick names, then you are the worst piece on the earth, and there is no use even if you get a huge name in society.

My guide

From childhood onwards I was reserved. After the 7th. I changed a bit in studies, and later on after eighth I changed a bit in nonsense. For every action there is an equal and opposite reaction; this is Newton's 3rd law. Similarly for every change there is a fellow behind us; this is nonsense law. And the fellow behind me was Vinod, from LKG to 10th he was my school mate. Until now he is the only one who has suffered my blows. Up to the 7th both of us had little rivalries, but after that we both got together. There were several similarities between the two of us; in the sixth class I got spectacles, and after that he also got spectacles. After ten years he removed the spectacles by surgery, and six months after his surgery I also kicked out my glasses. He was a little poorer in studies compared to me. I was happy over this. In the eighth class he came close. From then I started enjoying. I rode with him, I learned stealing from shops, I learned running. I crossed my street after he came. If he hasn't come into my life then I will be dumb forever. He showed the life in diagonal, I learned lot from him. But I never shared my personal matters with him; he didn't know about my crush and my fatty angel, and he didn't even know about my three angels.

He was quite cunning; he was too experienced in nonsense. An incident will explain about his nonsense. One day we both went to a fancy store to buy albums and he found one to his liking. He asked the price but the price was not within our reach. He started bargaining, but the shop keeper was not ready to reduce the price. He kept on bargaining but the shop keeper was not coming down. And now he started playing his skills. He said, "Anna, yesterday my sister bought this at a lower price from another fancy store, but here you are quoting a high rate."

Then the shop keeper said, "If you get this at a lower price from the other shop, I will give you two books for the price of a single one."

This was enough for him to show his skills, and it was enough for the shop keeper to be fooled by him.

My friend was a little mature in these things. He went to the next shop; I was not getting his plan, but I just followed his steps. In the next shop he got the album at the actual price, and here he worked on his plan. He asked the shop keeper to mention a lower price on the bill, and the shop keeper did as he asked. Now he had got the bill for the amount he wanted. I was surprised at his plan. With the lower price on the bill, we went to the previous shop and he showed the bill paper to the shop keeper. Not only was myself, the shop keeper also surprised now. He couldn't understand how this had happened, and he gave us two albums for the price of a single one.

This is a small example about him. He was too lazy a fellow, he was slothful.

Bill Gates said a few words about the lazy fellows,

"I like lazy fellows because they find easy ways to complete the work."

This I found in him.

He would try to solve a problem and a piece of work in the easiest way.

THE INCIDENT WHICH MADE ME SHOUTS ON MY FEAR.

This incident happened when I was in the 6th class. My friend brought a greeting card to school. All my friends were looking at it with much curiosity, and at last after a long while it came to my hands. I don't know who tore it, I'm an innocent guy, but now the torn greeting card was in my hands when he came for it. I said I'm not the one who tore it, but he didn't take my words, he blamed me, actually he knew that I hadn't done it, but he didn't have enough guts. So he caught me and asked for money.

He lacked courage, so he caught me, and I was speechless, so I got caught by him without any mistake on my part. He asked for money

I said ok. I didn't know the cost of the card, so I asked him how much. He mentioned the price, and on hearing the price my brain felt screwed.

"Damn! What?"

"Yes, it is costly. My dad brought it from Proddhutur," he cried.

Proddhutur is a big town which is half an hour from our town. I was hooked now; I didn't have enough money.

"Tomorrow I will pay," I said.

The next day I went to school with empty hands, he asked for money, he frightened me, I cried, and he left me and gave me another chance. It was not easy to earn that much money.

How?

Then I decided to take money from the suit case. Ya it was quite good; when my mom was out of the house I took the money and gave it to him. He was so clever, he had purchased for half the amount and he returned the remaining amount. Daily he did the same thing; I too liked this because every day I was enjoying the unexpected money. But my mom was not enjoying, everyday some amount was missing. Mom knew about the missing money, but she didn't scold me. What would she get if she beat me? Nothing. So mom made a plan to stop this.

She told me, "Arey nana, daily money goes missing from my suitcase, I don't know who is doing this. Do you know who is taking the money?"

"No ma, I don't," I said with innocent face.

"Ok nana, tomorrow a wizard is coming to our home to find out the missing money. He will find out who the thief is with some spiritual calculations," mom replied.

I was stunned.

"Ma what is it, is it necessary," I cried.

"Yes nana, it is necessary. Even lord Shiva can't find the thief."

"Ma, how will he find the thief ma?" I asked.

"He will do some pujas in our home, and he is a spiritual genius who knows everything; after the puja he will find out the thief," Mom replied.

"How will he find, ma?" I asked again.

"While doing the puja, the thief will get a horrible pain in the stomach and blood will come out from his mouth, and then he will fall down," she said.

I was frightened, I was going to get caught, and I would get a horrible pain.

No.

Shit of him (friend).

I didn't know what to do. Next day morning I woke up early. I didn't have enough guts to tell the truth. If I told mom, I didn't know how she would react. I went to school with a little tension. There he again asked for money. I said no, I don't have.

He asked again,

I said no I don't have.

He got angry and tried to frighten,

I knew what would happen if I took the money, so I didn't have options.

"I don't have money and from now I won't give you money, do as your wish." I shouted at him.

He was shocked at me; he walked away from there silently.

I went home for afternoon lunch. "Mom where is that wizard, has he found the thief," I asked.

"No, he didn't come today," mom said.

That bloody fear made me a thief, and that bloody fear made me courageous.

We don't get any courage from motivation or from anything else; we get it only from incidents or from situations. When mom talked about pujas and pain and blood, I was frightened. I feared how the situation would be if I was caught. Thinking about that situation I was frightened, and was shivering. I turned violent and I shouted at him.

We get pain only when we meet with an injury, without that we can't feel pain.

My schooling ended.

Twelve years from LKG to 10th standard.

My schooling started with "CRYING" and it ended with "SADNESS."

My school taught me so many lessons, from CRYING to SADNESS.

In between that happiness, little fights, scolding, less marks, worst malpractices, little robberies, girls, crushes, funny things, nick names, anger, and friends.

All the naughty stuff I learned in school.

I learned the meaning of laughing

I learned the meaning of fear

I learned the meaning of courage

School is the primary education for happiness and for everything. Here we learn so many things.

Along with six subjects we have one more important subject – it is enjoyment. No teacher is appointed for this subject; we have to learn it with our fellows.

Those days, that enjoyment… that never comes back.

It's a beautiful memory.

After the schooling our present enjoyment turns to past life's memory.

From now we feel the changes, first time my enjoyment moved to memories, and my present turned to past.

After twelve years I was moving to another home.

2008–2010

INTERMEDIATE

In the 10th class I got 63%, but I had expected 80%. 17% marks had gone from me. After getting my result I felt bad, because I didn't get 80%, I was still at 60%. Nothing had changed, and I was still there. There was no damn reason for me to change my studies. It was not the fault of reason, it was the fault of my attitude, my attitude was like that. At the time of the exams, my dad had said, "I trust u ra," but I didn't get good marks. I secured first class marks, I hadn't even moved up to 70%. On the results day I felt very bad. In the evening my dad came to me and said, "Arey stop your acting; I know about you, you are a 60% student, so don't expect more, ok, don't feel."

That's it.

My dad went out saying this.

Yes, I need not feel so much **because** I hadn't put in efforts for 80%, I just stopped at 60%. I stopped crying. I also went out. But I had killed my dad's hopes. While doing mistakes we don't think about our parents. In the 9th final exams, I had got 500 marks, but those were not mine, I had just rewritten the marks; but seeing it my dad increased his hopes on me. But now I had killed his hopes. And I didn't even have any answer for my dad's hopes.

Ok, doing mistakes and realizing our faults are the major attributes of kids, and soon my dad will also realize this.

The next step was that I wanted to join the intermediate (11th standard) course. I took M.P.C, i.e., the mathematical group. It was not my selection, my marks selected this group.

In our area our marks select our groups. And there is no chance for students to their interests and inclinations.

If a student is a good fighter in studies then he chooses science group, if a student is average in studies then he chooses mathematical group, and if a student is not good in studies then he chooses Arts group (social).

These are the common groups selected by students. No, not by students, by marks.

In some families not only marks, but parents also took a chance to decide the groups according to their interest, and they didn't even give a chance to their children.

In my home also the same process was done, but they chose the exact group for me. Actually I'm interested in science, and in case I had got the expected marks, then without any doubt I would have chosen the science group. But, for my brain, science is not the right group, and my cerebrum could not have adjusted with science. So I escaped from a big problem. If not, I would have been stuck in the intermediate class only. It would have taken some years for me to get a seat in medicine.

So I chose M.P.C. In the tenth I had got 80% marks in mathematics. I joined the local college. Before joining the local college I asked about corporate college, but dad refused it, and he joined me in the local college. I didn't get it and I didn't like it. We are totally four in my family, and my elder sister and my brother were far away from home, and now me and my younger sister were at home, so my dad was not interested in my joining a far away college. He wanted to keep me with him. So he joined me in the local college in Proddhutur.

Proddhutur is 30 minutes from our town. Along with me, my school mate also joined the same college, and same group, but in different section because of marks. Daily at 7 o' clock in the morning, we went by bus to college.

Now that I was going to college, I had thought big about the intermediate. I wished to join the corporate college far from town, but it did not happen, so I adjusted with the local one.

Daily going to college standing on footboards, feeling the fresh dusty air from the road, and little husky looks on girls… I felt as if I had got wings to fly.

I felt that I was mature.

But within days I was tired of this, day by day I was getting more tired and I was feeling bored.

And in intermediate every Sunday we have slip test and no rest at all. Every day study, study and study this is the only thing I found in college. And this was not co-educational college so no girls at all. And the college was in half acre and the classrooms are so strait. My school is far better when compared with the college.

I didn't adjust to the college atmosphere.

"Dad I don't like that college and the journey also, and I am not getting interest, so I don't want to go to that college, I want to join in our town," I said.

My dad didn't say anything.

On that day I didn't go to the college.

Mom was also not at home, she had gone to my aunt's town. In the evening when she came back, seeing me at home she asked about the reason for my holiday.

Then my dad said, "He didn't like that college and he wants to join in our town, so that's why he didn't go."

Saying truth is a logic trick.

"Arey we paid the fee, it's not refundable. And why don't you like that college ha, why don't you like, it's a good college, and before joining we had considered your decision also, so why are you behaving like this now."

And my mom became sentimental.

Hoo God!

What could I say now, mom was sentimental.

Now my dad entered into the conversation, "Hey Lakshmi what are you talking? From tomorrow onwards he will go to college; he wanted to take a holiday, so he just said like that, don't worry," my dad whispered.

Then I got my dad's intention; when I said I don't like college he didn't say anything to me.

What a plan he made!

"How God, how did you make dads so intelligent and moms so sentimental?"

What a plan my dad made. Because of moms, dads were becoming intelligent.

He succeeded with his trick.

From June to August were the daily routine days of college, no fun, no enjoyment, daily one hour's journey to college, I was tired of it. But some changes were waiting for me.

Our life was going to change in August.

Unforgettable month…

One of my cousins got married in August. August 13th was my last day in the college. We went to the marriage on August 14th, and we spent one week there. On August 22nd, early in the morning, myself, mom and my sisters returned to our town, but my dad and my brother did not come with us, they came in the afternoon. And the next day was Saturday. I woke up at college time, and Dad asked me, "Arey are you going to college or not." Next day was Sunday we had slip test in the college. So if I attended the college I had to write the slip exam the next day. How can I say to my dad that I don't want to go to college.

Then my brother said, "Arey if you go to college, tomorrow you have to attend the exam, so sit at home." Yes, that was correct; for the past seven days I hadn't gone to college, so I couldn't write the exam the next day.

"Well it's better to stay at home," I replied.

My dad looked at me.

I stayed at home, and in the evening my brother went to college and the next day was Sunday.

24 August 2008…

We didn't expect anything odd, but after getting them we didn't forget the odd happenings.

On that day my family went into silence, we missed our happiness, we didn't know what was going on. We waited for a miracle. But the miracle did not happen.

In the afternoon my mom and I went to the general store to buy some groceries, and after an hour we went back home. Buying chocolates or biscuits was common while we went shopping. That afternoon I bought some chocolates; sharing a chocolate or any snack item with my dad was very common in my home, my dad too used to ask for chocolates from us, so on that day I gave him a bite from the chocolate. My dad was sitting on the cot. He took one bite and he fell down, a paralytic stroke had attacked him.

At first I didn't know how to react. My mom ran towards my dad and immediately we took him to the hospital. The doctor suggested taking him to Proddhutur. We didn't understand anything, and then my relative Balaraj came to the hospital. My neighbor had informed to Balaraj about what had happened, so he immediately came to the hospital.

Balaraj, at the time of my dad's marriage was just a small kid. He had grown up in front of my parents, in our home.

Mom and I were in a stunned state. Balaraj arranged for a vehicle and talked with someone, and arranged everything, and we moved to Kurnool instead of Proddhutur. My elder and younger sisters came with us too. That was the first really dangerous situation I faced. On that day the auto driver charged fifty rupees for just a fifteen rupees journey. He charged three times what he actually should. From home to hospital was just a 10 minutes journey. But the auto driver charged fifty rupees. My weakness cost us fifty rupees. I gave him fifty rupees. It was not the time to bargain. Taking the fifty rupees, the auto driver said, "Babu, don't worry, dad will be alright." I surrendered to those words, words which cost fifty rupees.

"Situation never counts money, it counts emotions."

With the help of Balaraj, we went to Kurnool and we admitted him in a super specialty hospital.

Here I am thankful to Balaraj, without him I don't know how the day would have been.

After an hour my brother came from Kadapa. All my relatives came to Kurnool with pocket full. After two days my elder and younger sisters went to my aunt's home.

We were in that hospital for seven days, but there was no improvement. So my brother and my cousin Sashi decided to shift him to Hyderabad. My cousin worked hard to arrange for the shift. He thought ahead about the possible problems to make it easy.

After a week we moved from Kurnool to Hyderabad. On the seventh day in Kurnool my dad suffered a mild heart attack. Mom and my brother had gone home to get some documents and some money. My aunt, myself and my uncle were in the hospital. I could not make out what was going on, the nurses were running, and I thought that there was some serious problem. I too was running with shiver between the ICU and the medical shop. After an hour the doctors controlled the situation.

Ooff I relaxed.

I had seen a real dead end by then.

In the evening we shifted to Hyderabad, and there dad fought for life for three weeks. Twenty-nine days after the stroke my dad quit his life. My dad left his life after sixty years. My home has changed a lot since then. My dad quit his life without seeing our life.

My dad never taught me anything,

But I learned a lot from him.

A great incident with my dad…

When I bought anything I spent more money when compared to others. One day my mom got angry with me.

"You are wasting a lot of money, when you earn yourself then spend as you like, but now try to control," she said. On that day I didn't even ask her for a coin, but how could I manage without junk food, so I went direct to my dad and I asked him for a coin. My dad gave me a coin and then I asked, "Dad am I wasting money?"

While giving the coin my dad gave a tremendous reply, "Arey when I was a kid, we didn't have coins to buy snacks or anything. Our dad didn't have money to feed us with coins, so my brother and I earned coins to get such stuff and for our studies. But now you don't have that problem; for whom am I earning money? It is for all of you. I am earning for your sake not for my sake. I'm earning for your happiness, so you are spending your own money, go ahead and enjoy it."

When he cares for me he is my hero, when he scolds he is my villain. I saw both hero and villain in him.

For my sake he joined me in tuition,

For my sake he beat me,

For my sake he made me everything.

"I never changed my path while walking with my dad."

"He just walked with me."

"He is responsible, so he beats me for my nonsense."

"He is a father, so he says sorry to me after his anger wears off."

"It's enough to say about my dad."

"I get everyday share from his money and he also gets his share from our chocolates."

In the 10th class once my dad beat me. After a long time he beat me again and it was the last time that he got angry with me.

Every day my younger sister and I used to with fight each other, it was quite common for us. In every home you will see this type of nonsense. In my home also the same nonsense used to take place. That day while eating, we both started fighting. Dad was watching and my sister was shouting. Seeing this, my dad's irritation went to its peak. I was sitting beside him and doing this nonsense. He lost his patience and gave a blow on my back. "Shut up," he shouted.

I went to bed without having my food, and then my mom started scolding. My sister also asked, "Dad, why did you beat him, we were just fighting each other, it's bad, dad."

My dad was stunned.

In the morning when I woke up at 7 o' clock my dad came towards me, and said "Sorry ra nana."

What?

My dad said sorry, from first slap to the last slap, days have changed and emotions have also changed.

Mom shows enormous love for us. Dad shows enormous responsibility to us. Saying sorry to son, really dads are great yaar.

We just walk with them but they hold our hand to help us from taking wrong steps; when we take wrong steps, they warn us. If we do something wrong even after this, they still come with us for support. Don't know how they feel while first taking us in their hands, but from then onwards they never leave us, they take care all the time.

When I lost my father I just cried only for ten minutes, never after that. My dad's death taught me a lesson. How to live, how to survive, who are ours and who are not. From these lessons we have to learn how to live, how to survive, who are ours and who are not; from every negative impact we should find some positive direction, so you should just feel and not be afraid of them. Nothing is going to happen. Just learn some stuff from this.

When you face a problem automatically you learn how to overcome it, and how to survive from that, so there is no need to get any indirect motivation from outside.

After this situation mom took up the responsibility. Every month mom used to take money from dad's pocket to buy groceries, but now she had to spend money from her pension. She got this responsibility. A huge change occurred.

"My mom was fantastic. No words to say anything more. Without her my dad was not a hero and not a villain." And we are nothing.

Moms were always super.

After that my brother also entered into the responsibilities. Until now studies alone played a key role in his life, but from now on responsibilities also became a part of his life. He was not a wonderful person earlier. But after this situation his care and responsibilities made him wonderful. Until now he had to bother only about himself, but now he had to look after the whole family. Earlier he had to attend only his friends' calls, but now he had to take all calls, he had to answer every question, and he had to run the family. And he was the answer for every question. More than mom his life had changed a lot.

What can we give him in return for his caring and for his responsibility?

"Respecting him and standing beside him is the only thing we have to give."

One thing I appreciate – Brahma made elders to be a little courageous. It's true.

"I don't know how he was before, but now he is not as he was before."

Now he became responsible.

At the time when my dad was in hospital, I and my younger sister changed our college and school, we both shifted to Anantapur. And the reason for this shifting was because of my dad, we thought that our dad would get cured and then he would need physiotherapy treatment for paralysis. There were no physiotherapy doctors in our town, so we wanted to move to Proddhutur, as dad would require physiotherapy every day. Proddhutur was a little far from town and no one would be at home, all were studying far away from town, and it was not easy for mom all by herself, so we decide to transfer. So both of us joined there. We had relatives there. But after that my dad expired.

We couldn't go back to our town thereafter, as we had both joined in college and school. Mom couldn't stay alone, so for our sake my mom also came with us.

My dad was a Central Government employee. After his demise, mom got dad's pension. In the beginning, although we got less amount of pension, we lived our life happily. It was because of my mama, mom's brother, because of whom we survived happily.

And now about myself… in the middle of the academic year I had joined the local college. The first year of my intermediate course was not good because the first half of it I had studied in Proddhutur, and the second half I studied in Anantapur. From September I didn't go to college also. So no enjoyment and no studies in the first year, and I failed in two subjects. I felt very bad, as for the first time I failed in the public exam. It was the worst that I had faced. I am average in studies, but failing in subjects is not my thing either, so I felt very bad. But no one scolded me because of the situation. I completed the failed subjects in the supplementary examination. In the first year I got 71 percent.

This year was the worst year for me, not only me, for the entire family.

In this year I understand lots of things.

SECOND YEAR OF INTERMEDIATE...

For the second year of intermediate I changed to another college. It was because of my results. Actually I had got good marks; I got 71% in the first year, but my parents were expecting more from me. So they joined me in another college.

In second year another college, another atmosphere, but here I was one of the top students in the last section. In this last section all were duller when compared with me, so obviously I was the topper candidate. And college was also not fair, every Sunday they held weekend tests. Actually the entire intermediate course is not a good one. It's like hell... here we had to study all the time. I was tired of these rules. At 8 o' clock in the morning we had to attend college, and if we went a minute late then the teachers sent us out.

Time sense, punctuality, what nonsense is all this… this is a worse nonsense than our nonsense. I was fed up with this, so every Saturday personally I took holiday. In the second year I enjoyed a little better when compared to the first year. And my study was also the same as the first year. In every weekend test I got good marks, but in mathematics I got a little less. In the intermediate I had chosen mathematics but I was not good at mathematics. Mathematics was the subject in which I had failed in the first year. It was as if I don't know swimming but I had jumped into water. I tried a lot for my final exams. But this year again I failed in one subject. Now this was really the worst thing in my life; again I had failed in one more subject. Looking at myself in the mirror I spat at my image lots of times. Shit, what worst thing I am, in my family no idiot failed in the exams. I was the first person to fail in my family. In the 10th every one thought that I was going to be the top scorer in our family, but I went to the least scorer, and now I had failed in subjects. In the first year I had some reason, but now there was no such problem, and even then I kicked one subject. I was ashamed of myself, but no one scolded me.

I completed that subject in supplementary examination. When I think about that subject, I feel fully ashamed of myself. Studying is the easiest thing and intermediate is dead easy and as for me I have capability. Four years back I had learned how to study, and yet I failed. In weekend tests I was a good fellow, but now I had failed in a subject. If you study at least important questions you can easily survive, but I flopped.

And after that I joined coaching for Eamcet (Engineering and Medicine common entrance test). I didn't know whether

I would get good scores in Eamcet. But I wanted to at least qualify in Eamcet, if not I was not eligible for engineering.

I went for Eamcet coaching in our college, I didn't have much hope.

I took the exam and after a couple of weeks I got the results. I had qualified in Eamcet exam. Now I was going to join engineering.

Thank you God.

After I flopped in the intermediate I thought a lot about my career, and finally I got the solution that I'm not interested in studies, I am interested in some other thing. I said so to my mom, but mom regretted it and she conveyed it to my brother.

He said to me, "Now you are frustrated, so you are thinking that you are not good in studies. First complete your engineering, and even after that if you find that you are interested in the same passion, then move on to your passion."

Sounds good to hear, so I accepted his advice. Now I didn't know how to move into my passion and I didn't have an option. If I tried to move towards my passion, there was no one to accept it, and no one was prepared to send me also. So it was not the right time to fight. So silently I joined engineering, thinking that in case after four years I'm still interested in the same thing, then we will see.

Intermediate results made me a little curious about my passion.

So engineering was the test center for my passion.

Engineering counseling: I went with my brother for my counseling. While we were waiting in the waiting hall, my brother spoke to me about the IIT. He explained a lot about that. Why was he explaining about it, this was not the time because I had just completed my intermediate (12th standard), and I had attempted the state level engineering test, and I was here for counseling, now this fellow is talking about IIT. Why?

What is the use?

He is trying to motivate, so I remained silent.

After an hour the counseling was over, and after a couple of days I placed web options for some specified colleges according to my eligibility criteria. After some days the allotment was released and I got a seat in another district. I was happy, and everyone was happy except for one person.

My brother was not happy. After my allotment he made a call and asked, "Arey why are you going to second counseling?"

What?

"Who said so," I asked.

"Vinod told me," he replied.

Then I understood his words. I hadn't spoken to Vinod and he didn't know about my allotment, then how could Vinod say anything about my second counseling? But here my brother was saying so. He was behaving like my father. I got the situation. After my 10th my dad had also behaved in the same pattern. When I told my dad that I wished to join a corporate college, he didn't send me out of town. Here my brother also was not ready to send me out, so he was speaking like that. Very soon I got what was in his mind, and I decided to go for second counseling. It was not a right time to move out.

In second counseling I got a seat in the local college which was near home. I joined civil engineering, of which I didn't know even the spelling. One crazy scene happened after I joined; my uncle asked me what is ECE Ok I knew about it, and I said ECE is a branch which deals with electrical and communication engineering. After that he asked what EEE is. Now I was stuck. I didn't know about this. I murmured and I gave a nonsensical answer. That was my situation. In that bloody situation I joined engineering.

The last two years had taught me a lot. Personal to professional, I learned a lot in these two years. I was not big enough to understand the situations, but the situation made me understand, and I started getting the situations.

In these two years I was far from enjoyment, it was a little scary how I completed these two years. In these years I got the meaning of life.

"Life is like this."

"Life can change with emotions."

I found who are ours and who are not.

More than me my brother got a lot of understanding in these two years.

After losing something, definitely we gain something.

Here I gained life,

Value of life,

Meaning of life,

Life is crazy, it has no limits.

We wish for something and life wishes something else, in between we war fared with life.

But definitely we get something.

2010–2011

ENGINEERING FIRST YEAR

My engineering… my college life had started; I entered into professional studies.

It was time to enjoy, no restrictions, no lock on our freedom and moreover no need to fight with books. It all depends on us; if we feel bored then we look at the book to get some relaxation. These things I noticed from others and from movies. Before joining the college my brother had also spoken about college life and how it should be.

I entered into enjoyable days.

With lots of hope we entered college. But the college presented something beyond the limits of what we expected. Every college should be like this. At first I didn't like my college and its atmosphere, but later I became addicted to it.

My college is spacious, extending to nearly fifty acres. And our college is 40 km from our town and 3 km from a town called Gooty. And there is no compound wall for our enjoyment. And we moved in college buses to the college.

After getting a seat, my brother and I went to college to take admission and to submit my allotment orders and certificates. My sister-in-law also works in the same college and was placed in the college placement cell. She explained in detail about my principal and his strictness.

The first time I met him in the office room, he asked my allotment order and checked my allotment. He then spelled out his rules, not his rules the college rules. But it seems to be like as his rules. Hearing his words I didn't have any hope of girls, enjoyment and absenteeism. Actually with this type of principal no student can enjoy his college life. I shivered, but for me from childhood I had been escaping from strictness.

About my principal: He was very strict, and if he got angry he started looking like Rudhrudu. All were equal in his eyes, he did not discriminate between lecturers and students, all were the same to him, and he didn't show any difference. This was a good quality he had; if a student got less marks he tore his skin, and if any lecturer didn't show good performance in teaching then he did the same thing for him also. And he is little temper. I liked this quality in him, it's the best quality he had. He was a very good and fine principal. He was principal for the students, and not for the college; he stood on behalf of students, not lecturers. Lots of fellows were beaten by him but no one hated him.

"Even I also took a part of his anger."

This is the feedback on my principal.

At first I didn't understand him, I feared him. Later I grasped the college atmosphere. Actually at first all the fellows didn't do any nonsense; initially they were quiet, but after getting the college atmosphere then they started their activities. At first I was a good kid in classes.

With fear I entered the college.

First day of my college.

I was waiting for my college bus; at 8:30 am I got into the bus. I was feeling a little scared about ragging but I escaped from it. I didn't know anyone in the bus, so I took a corner seat and non-teaching staff were also present in the bus. So no ragging took place in the bus. The principal too had made strict rules against ragging. So there was no ragging in the bus. Some of my classmates were also there in my bus, but I didn't know them.

I reached college. I knew just a single fellow there, he was Sudheer and we called him as psycho. He was my cousin's friend. He received me and our right hands joined in a warm handshake. We both went to our class room. He started talking about the college and the class room, but within a minute I had reached the class room. It was looking like a 'Saturday market'. In our town on 'Saturday market' all the villagers came to the town with their goats and buffalos to sell them. Our class room was looking like that. Both mechanical and civil fellows were combined in the room. And the noise sounded like a group of honey bees seeking the hive. All were totally in a noisy mood; it was a 2 cent width class room in which the sounds were reflecting from one end to the other end.

I entered the noisy room, no one was bothering me, as they were in their element, and all benches were filled with noisy guys. I found a place on the back bench and went to take a seat. And I found another friend on the last bench. He introduced himself, he stated his name and his branch, and he belongs to the mechanical branch.

And I introduced myself,

Then another one from the front bench turned towards me, and introduced himself saying,

"Hey I'm also from civil, and my name is Venkata Rami Reddy."

I introduced myself.

He was the first person from my branch who introduced himself to me.

After an hour our class had dispersed, and the two branches were separated. Two branches were allotted two class rooms. We moved to our class and mechanical guys moved to their class room.

After the first counseling, college had started, but I entered after the second counseling, so introductions had already been completed. So when we entered the class room no introduction was held. With a little confusion I sat on the second bench with Sudheer. I'm feeling like a stranger in the class room. Some of the fellows were making jokes, some were making nonsense and some were shouting, but I was sitting like a garden lizard on a stone and watching them like a stranger.

At the afternoon me, Sudheer and another fellow went for lunch. I introduced and he too introduced his self.

He was Mr. Romantic, a romantic fellow, romantic king of our class. Not only our class, he was romantic king for the whole college. He was naughty with his words. We three completed our lunch. At lunch we three had a chat about the subjects.

The strange thing is, in the beginning we spoke about studies before discussing other activities, but later, after getting introduced to the other activities we never spoke about subjects. If anyone disturbed our conversation with studies we scolded them; only students can behave so strangely.

In the initial days I ran around the college with Mr Romantic. I bunked classes for the first time with him. Goody friendly fellow, the whole class laughed on hearing his words. From him I started understanding characters and attitudes.

In the college we learn something which makes us everything.

I learned something from him which is the starting step to get everything. A percentage of something learned from him. One of the best fellows, who was liked by the whole class… He was the laughter medicine of our class, everyone enjoyed his company. Not only his words, his laughable jokes also were romantic and his communications skills were so nice. He was the best communicator of our class. Once he experimented his skills on our principal, who didn't get his words and was shocked.

But later principal also fell in love with him.

He was that good,

In the evening on our college bus I met a guy who was my class mate. And I called him Aza.

A class room is filled with people of different types of attitudes and he was one among them. I liked him well. He was one among the characters whom I liked in my class.

In the evening while travelling on my college bus, one of my seniors said something about the subjects, which I couldn't understand. He was spelling it out, and I asked what it was, and he replied "Don't you know?"

I didn't give any answer, then this thin fellow entered into our conversation and he covered up for my ignorance. I saw him with a simple smile on his lips, which seemed to reflect his nature, and we started introducing each other.

I had seen him in class room, but he hadn't seen me. So when I said that I was also in the civil engineering branch, he tried to recollect. But he couldn't remember me.

He didn't know me, but yet he entered into conversation, which was a measure of his character. That very minute we became friends.

He was a thin fellow with zero size structure, no girl could give better competition to his structure. And he was too noisy; no noisy fellow could be a competitor for him, fully loaded with noise as he was. He was the first person who was caught by the principal and he was also the first one to started fighting with other branch guys. He was a part of every college fight.

Good fellow with good attitude.

"Good first day."

On the first day itself I met a supportive guy.

For the most part of my college days, I walked with him, and a good number of cigars we lit with each other.

In the second year we both bunked more classes than the cigars we lit, from year to year we grew closer.

"In B.Tech I met a good friend."

The first day in the morning I was scared about the college. I didn't know how it would be, but by the evening I feel good, now I had three friends, Sudheer, Mr. Romantic and Aza.

Now to another one…

After two days during the lunch break, a giant character came with us for lunch. I was frightened on seeing him. He was 6.2 feet tall and 90 kg in weight. He looked like the father of our class, his structure frightened us but his attitude was not like his physique.

He was the daddy of our class.

He was of a totally different attitude, he was too joyous. His attitude dominated his physique.

"A giant man with jocular attitude" – an interesting combination.

During the lunch break we got introduced to each other. Sudheer and daddy were from the same school, so they already knew each other. When for the first time I sat beside him he started making jokes on others and on me also. I looked at him, again he made another joke on me, and next time I didn't look at him, but he was not stopping. He was behaving like my close friend. Just a couple of hours back we had met each other, but within hours he became close to me but I'm not, and he was even playing jokes on me. Before becoming a friend first we become as a class mate, after that we turn to friends, but this giant fellow was not like others. Every class mate may or may not turn to be a friend, but daddy made everyone his friend. His behavior was such. Every fight, every function, had him in it. He was the back bone of joy.

At first I didn't react well to his jokes but later I changed.

He was too gutsy. He was full of fun all the time, and noisy too; my entire class was filled with noisy guys.

From then to now he hasn't changed his jokes on us.

I enjoyed my days with him, with his attitude and with his gutsy physique.

I missed the days of enjoyment without him.

And about fighting, he played an important role in this, but he tried to compromise all the time.

Every class needs this type of character.

His jovial nature and his attitude and presence of nature made him little different.

In my entire engineering career, I never saw him angry.

And another character who influenced me…

A temperamental character. I liked his attitude most. If I had a chance to change my attitude, I would choose his attitude. A rebellious attitude, I liked his arrogance very much. No stepping back for him. He was the first person who raised his voice before the principal. From my first day onwards I had been seeing him. During my first days I thought that he was reserved but he was not. We both got into the same bus at the same stop. The first two days I didn't watch him in the class, but later I caught him in the class room. In the beginning I hesitated a little to speak with him, but later he came close to me in the class. He was noisier than the others, no one could control his noise. When I try to compare him from the first day up to now, nothing has changed. From childhood he was noisy.

I saw him first on the first bench; he had logic for the bench selection. When a student opts for the last bench, the lecturers think that he would be a noisy candidate, if a student takes a place in the middle, then all the lecturers ask questions to them only, so the lecturers concentrate less on the first bench students, and they never ask questions also. For this reason he chose the first bench. He was a cold blooded intellectual fellow. But later he shifted to the second bench and then to the third bench and at last he chose the last bench, and after that he kicked the class room. Too different attitude he has.

He was too good at studies, but these types of guys never take studies seriously, they just kick it, because they know what it is like.

His communication skills on problems and his rationale to deal with problems were nice. He deals with everything as if it was simple. He knew where to stop and where to start.

He was also like my principal in that he didn't show any difference between teachers and friends; all were equal for him. Nothing and no lecturer frightened him. He only frightened them lot of times.

Once he teased me badly, but after that he asked,

And I was frightened by his behavior. In school days I was frightened by Sri Kanth now here he frightened me.

Later in the evening he asked "Arey did you feel badly?"

In friends we found this interesting thing at first they tease us and later they asked arey mama did you feel bad.

Idiotic questions.

I said, "No ra."

And another character…

A riotous kid, most noisy one, without him no riot would be held. He was our class C.R. and also our cricket team captain. He was our gang leader and class leader. No one spoke like him. Strongly I can say he is the only one who can survive anywhere under any condition. He could get anything he wanted. If he got less attendance, he would talk his way through to get full attendance, if he got less marks, with his words he would manage to get full marks. He can change every situation to his convenience, and he moulds every one. He was the only one who qualified in GATE entrance exam from our college. Without him no noise ever happened.

About his studies: His studies were also like his words. He always bunked classes with us, he ran around the college with us, and he lit cigars with us. He bunked as many classes as all of us, but he was still clearing the subjects. From the first year to final year he didn't flop in a single subject, and every semester he completed all subjects at a time. . Very few students completed their subjects without failing in a single subject, and among those intellectual fellows he was one.

At first I was not good at talking, I used less words with friends. One day we changed the college bus, all these fellows went to another bus, and I too went with them; but I didn't get a seat and I adjusted with those fellows, they were all playing jokes on each other, and I was enjoying the jokes, but I didn't make any jokes. Then Aza raised his voice, "Arey why are you silent? Speak some words, ra come close to us," he shouted.

Then this fellow entered into the conversation, and said, "Arey first tease him or play a joke on him, automatically he will come close to us."

I was stunned at his words, he knew how to make friends.

Really interesting fellow he was.

Every kid is a little riotous, but he was a little more than that. And he was a tutor to rascals and he made all of us riotous too. The whole college knew about him, every person from watchmen to principal. He was involved in every fighting, meaning our branch fighting, and he was the leader there too. He was one with an identity. He was a good nasty fellow, good noisy guy.

I liked these guys' attitudes, this fantastic four were involved in every fight. Principal used to call these fellows if any nonsense happened in our branch.

All of us travelled by the same bus, but I was not like these guys. I liked these guys' attitudes most. Everyone was different and everyone was a little nasty.

After a couple of weeks of our introduction, our seniors held a fresher's day. Now we had to interact with the seniors. From the first day onwards ragging was not going on. But in the fresher's day they got a right to tease us and to rag. No principal and no lecturers came between us, it was their day.

On the fresher's day morning in our bus for first time in my life, I had the experience of ragging. Ragging, which is an introduction between juniors and seniors... By this a physical bond occurs between us. I had watched this in lots of movies, and I felt a little curious and little excited. And in the bus one of my seniors asked for my bio-data, and I replied in short terms. That's it, he didn't ask any extra questions, it was over, very simple. I was shocked. This was the worst ragging I experienced.

I expected more, but here no one knew how to do that also.

Shit.

If there is no ragging then there is no need to study in college. It's a superb experience, and if we miss it, then what is the use of studying in college.

And I am now thinking about fresher's day and about the ragging in the college. Because already I experienced worst ragging in bus. And in college also if it would be same then no worst thing can happen over than this.

And the function has started. My HOD and my principal make their speeches, and some of the lectures also shared their thoughts with us.

On the fresher's day my HOD also gave a speech; he was a fine and good HOD He had completed PhD and was multi talented. His speech said that he was very strict, but his way of teaching and behaving indicated that he was calm. After these speeches ragging started, one by one the senior were selecting the students and started ragging.

One of my seniors called me and asked for my bio-data. I gave an answer

And he asked who my favorite hero was,

I gave my favorite hero's name,

Then my senior asked, show how your hero walks.

I walked like him.

And asked about heroine, I gave my answer.

There are two heroines with the same name. One is in the south one heroine is in Bollywood. They thought I was talking about the South Indian heroine. Immediately I said, "Sir she is not the South Indian one, she is the North Indian heroine." My answer was good but the way I conveyed it was bad.

And they started; they asked why I liked her.

She was beautiful and her acting looks awesome so I like her. Here I used some decent words without making any vulgarity. But seniors got my point and asked some vulgar questions about her.

"Hoo what?"

"Don't you get my question, what is the feature you like in her?" One of my seniors shouted.

"Sorry sir, ya I got it but, but…" I murmured.

They didn't leave me, they asked another question.

What?

It was a little worse than the previous question. I didn't give any answer. How could I?

"No sir, I like her acting that's it," I replied.

They made another question

"Why do you keep your hands in the pocket while introducing yourself on the stage?" One of the senior asked.

"Sir, I don't know, without my involvement my hands pick my pocket sir," I replied.

"Aha, ok now with involvement say about your heroine."

Again he asked the same question.

"Sir, I just like her, that's it," I said.

No, say why you like her.

God they were not leaving me. "I wish to go sir," I murmured.

They looked at me a little awkwardly.

And they sent me off.

Hoo god I escaped from them, with these bloody questions my heroine was getting the worst because of them. I didn't like this.

Damn! I escaped without any answer. Then another senior pointed at me and called. God, again I'm going to be caught with nonsense questions.

Then one of the lecturers came and said, "Ya, party is completed; now you guys have to leave."

Hoo God, I escaped. And ok with ragging. Ragging doesn't mean making questions and giving answers; it means that seniors have to stultify juniors. I expected more but they stopped with questions.

And I'm ok with ragging. And I satisfied.

No one cried on fresher's day.

Now about my lecturers in the first year... not only in the students even in lectures also we find different attitudes.

We had a subject called mechanics. This was deal with by Sreenivasu sir, his teaching was a little different. More than the formulae he used the word "yes."

Yes have you completed the problem?

Yes, your attendance please, yes.

He used the word like this, but his teaching was good and he made it a little interesting. He spent 40 minutes in the class teaching the subject, and the remaining 15 minutes for entertainment.

And another sir, he dealt with physics. A systematic professor, he was said to be reserved, and even the principal never blamed him. He was the perfect professor for teaching and for jokes also. And his teaching was such that no notes were required.

In the first year we had seven subjects and five labs. Heavy numbers of subjects never scared me. In the intermediate we had only six subjects. So when I compared with this, nothing seemed bad. I know studying is easy, but making a space to study is not an easy thing for me. It's ok.

In the first year all the benches were filled with students, and there were only few absentees. Every day in the class room I thought about the subjects I had to study; I had to complete my graduation within the 4 years. I didn't know whether I could or not, but blindly I made a wish, blindly I thought about that. And a major cause for making the blind wish was my family. My brother was in medicine, and my elder sister was doing Ph.D, and my younger sister was too good in studies. Her wish was to become a doctor, no doubt she would made her wish come true. So blindly I too made my wish. I also wanted to be good in graduation. In intermediate I kicked subjects but here I need not be like that. I kept a target that without losing any month I have to clear my graduation within the time.

With this wish I completed a month, and our first mid exams started. Until now I had only thought about my wish, but I hadn't even started.

First mid had started, it was a funny first mid exam. Here some had friends and some did not. If a guy didn't know anything then he chose a friend to get some help, but some fellows didn't have any touch with other guys and for them the situation turns wild. In the examination hall some were looking for helpers and some didn't get any idea, because they didn't know whom to ask, or who was good and who was bad. Here every fellow could be dull and every fellow could be a clever one. And some fellows got help from others and they became friends after the exams. So don't make it late; on the very the first day you have to make friends, you never know how the situation will be.

We have to believe one thing here, there is a cause and there is a reason for every action. Not only for the life partners, even for becoming friends also there is a certain time and place required to meet a friend. And on that day I found that even exams are also causes for getting new friends.

My first mid was completed, I got good scores in some subjects and bad scores in some subjects. But the principal didn't accept it, so again we had to write the exam and we had to get good marks. Again I wrote the exam.

Totally I was a little blanked out in the first year.

After three months we got another mid exam. In between the first and second mid exams, nothing changed in studies, same routine marks and routine exams continued. And every day I was getting introduced to a new fellow. At the time of the second mid exams a group was introduced to me.

During the time of this mid exam, the whole class met a beautiful 80 kg guy named Suri.

Everyone gets close by an incident or by accident. He also came close to us by an incident. He came into focus at the mid exams time with his mischievous behavior. His behavior seems to be a little countrified. His slang and his words were more beautiful than him.

In a computer lab, another sexiest and stylish fellow came close to me. Every day he appeared with a new style of beard, he was the brand ambassador for style. And he had a separate saloon shop for himself, for his style.

Day by day one by one were growing close to me.

And day by day the college also moved. There was no enjoyment, and my first year moved forward strongly. In the first year I was not fully addicted to college, to studies and to bunking classes. Only introductions happened in the first year – character to character, attitude to attitude, subjects to subjects, lecturers to lecturers and a big introduction to the college atmosphere.

From the first year onwards I became a little irregular to college. In the first year I got 72 percent attendance.

This was the only semester where I didn't have to pay any condonation fee for attendance.

During the last month of the academic year, we had a college day function. So before the function the college conducted lots of games, both indoor and outdoor.

We participated in all games like cricket, kabadi and volley ball. But we didn't hit a single prize. It was because we were freshers, and another reason was that we didn't give better performance. And I didn't play games. But I enjoyed games, and more than that I enjoyed the commentary. The commentary should be racy and spell-binding, and we can't enjoy the game without commentary. And our commentary was more interesting than the game. Even Harsha Bhogle couldn't beat our commentary. Not only international matches, even street matches also need commentary, but a little wild commentary.

And our commentary should be a little funny, "Arey play like this, like that, go, go, go catch the ball, shit hoo oo, you missed it, easy catch man, arey stupid shooting is not going, here don't make stills hit the ball, ok ok cool, chill man," and arguing with the umpire, "No it's out he didn't touch the line." In our matches no third umpire was present so we got into fighting. We even scolded the umpire. "No umpire is cheating, he is favoring them, no you guys are cheating the players, and leg umpire is not noticing we want to change the umpire," and at last it leads to fighting with the opposite team's players, and then the principal or any other higher authority had to come to solve the problem.

Nothing went wrong in the stadium; it was we who made good things wrong.

And we motivated our mates also like, "Arey your girl friend is watching, hit the boundary," and if he hit we changed the words to, "Arey we know ra she is watching you that's why you hit the boundary na, arey if you made lead runs I will buy you a beer," and we called them by using nick names. And we motivated them with our commentary. We didn't know whether we would win or not, but we made commentaries. No game ended without a commentary.

We lost all the games, but we didn't miss the enjoyment. We enjoyed lot.

And next was the college day function, My friends had talked about the college day, that in the function lots of riots will happen and unseen things will happen in the class rooms, and that there would be a high level of security.. Hoo, hearing this really I was a little curious on that day. But on the day I didn't find any nonsense. I wandered through all the rooms of the college, but I didn't find even a tiny fighting or censored scenes either. The next day some fellows talked about fighting and the censored scenes, "Arey we watched this, and we watched that."

I didn't get how they found these things and why I couldn't find those things. I didn't get this. I didn't get whether they are saying true or false.

But in the function we shouted like hell, our throats went hoarse. Afterwards we relaxed and went for dinner, and we filled our bellies and went back.

And at last my first year came to an end, totally seven subjects and five labs. I had to complete all these subjects and labs. And we had to write lab records. No one wrote their class works but everyone has to place their pens on their records. And we wanted to impress the lecturers. If the lecturers got good impressions, then they used red inked pen well. So a little nervous and worried, I completed my labs external exam.

Out of the seven subjects I liked only one, physics. I liked that subject because of the lecturer. His teaching was amazing; my principal too liked his teaching. He taught in a professional manner and was my favorite lecturer.

I had a innocent experience with him.

It was a McKenna's Gold experience with him.

Along with the theory of the subject we had a physics lab as well. He dealt with both subject and lab.

In the lab we had to do ten experiments. Every week we did one and we took correction from him. On the day of the exam, all of us had to submit our records and practical note books. On the day before the exam, he said that he would give marks according to our experiments. In total there were ten, and I had done only nine experiments. I would hence get fewer marks in practical, so I made a plan. I had done nine experiments only, and in the practical book also I had written only nine experiments, but I wanted to make it ten. I got an idea. I wrote the last experiment in the note book, and I corrected it myself and I signed like him.

During the practical exam I showed him the book, but he was too intelligent and he caught me on seeing his signature,

He asked, "Who made this sign?"

"You only sir," I replied.

He looked at me, my face was innocent.

But he was too confident about his signature, so he checked the date.

Here he caught me, because under the signature he always wrote the date also, and I had also written the date. But the only mistake I made was that the date I had written was a Sunday. Not even a working day…

He looked at me, and showed pity on my innocence.

He didn't scold me, I am the worst among the worst.

"Arey you didn't do the experiment, look at them. All are doing the experiment, why don't you join with them and why don't you complete it? I gave a chance to them," he shouted at me.

Shit, what?

He had given a chance, I didn't know about this,

What's wrong with me, if I had gone with nine, nothing was wrong in that. But my bloody brain made a mistake, it forced me to do something wrong.

I bent my head in shame.

Caught by any nonsense is good to face. But here I was caught by mistake, silly mistake; even a school student won't do this type of mistake. But I did that.

By catching me with the silliest mistake, he concluded that I was the most innocent fellow in the civil branch. He gave me good marks in the practicals.

Yes I'm an innocent fellow. Not only in the studies, but even in other area so many mistakes had I made.

One of my mistakes…

Once I went to a grocery shop to buy eggs, and the shop owner gave me a cover and said take six eggs. Then I thought why don't I try to take seven eggs instead of six. Good idea I had.

I took seven eggs and I gave money for six eggs only. I went home. In the teen age we feel a little proud while doing mistakes, and at that age we feel that such mistakes are our own property. I opened the cover and in that I found only five.

What the heck?

I didn't get anything.

I was stunned.

I had taken only five.

While taking the eggs I thought to take seven, but I took only five and I gave money for six eggs.

Immediately I ran to the shop to get one more egg. And I bought one more egg.

I told this to my mom, and she laughed at me. Mistakes are our special properties, so we have to take care while doing such acts, or else your property will be confiscated.

Concentration is important while doing such small deceptions.

So when you want to do mistakes just think once, because you may even lose what you should get.

I did the same mistake in the record book.

But later in the external exam, I failed in this same subject.

My lab externals were completed and I got good marks in all the lab externals.

Now it was time for the main exams. Up till now I didn't know what I had studied and what I had learned, but here I wished to complete in time. Out of these seven subjects two were mathematical subjects and my fate turned back. All the five labs had not scared me because labs are in lecturer's hands, so there was no need to worry, but these two subjects made me worry. One major advantage was that we wrote our exams in our own campus, and now we were a little close to one another, so without any shame we could easily mingle with the mates to get answers. During the external exams I found some of my class mates whom I had never found in the class till then. At the end of the first year of B.Tech, I saw some of my fellows for the first time.

My first year ended.

I had written the exams well, but I was a little worried about one subject, i.e., Drawing. For civil students this subject is very important.

This was dealt with by Manan.

In the first year he showered his total crossness on me.

For anything that happened in the class room, the only name he called was mine. I don't know whether he didn't know the other names or not, but he would call only one name.

"You get up and say this answer."

"You get up and do this."

"Where are your drawing sheets, what have you done, do it, I want it now. Tomorrow you have to complete it."

In the drawing room he showed me hell.

I didn't do anything to him and I am not a nonsense kid, then why was he doing like this and showing his crossness to me.

If I get a chance I wish to become a lecturer and I want him as my student. This was the only wish I made in every drawing period.

For three hours I fought with my watch. And I was ready to kick my shoes.

But the little happiness in this was that I don't have any lab for drawing. I escaped from that.

If it had been there, I don't know how the situation would be.

With little enjoyment I completed my first year. In the first year I enjoyed very little. At the start I didn't get how to accept my engineering life, and I didn't know how to enjoy engineering.

I was in engineering. My brother was correct. My engineering was like what they had said, but for me it took a little time to mingle.

My first year was a little boring. I didn't understand the subjects, but even then I stick to the bench to understand something but no answer injected. Lots of fun was going on outside, but I did not take part in it.

"Unsettling subjects, limited marks and total dilemma in the first year."

2011–2012

SECOND YEAR

I completed my first year with 72% attendance and in that I enjoyed only 20% and the remaining I spent in the class room.

In the second year I moved little closer to my class mates, and I moved a little close to enjoyment, and enjoyment also liked me so it also came close to me. And here I learned some new habits. Until now I used to feel a little tense while doing mistakes, and my hand would shiver, but now I was ready and my hand was ready to do mistakes. And I started bunking classes and I started enjoying my engineering life. My enjoyable days started.

Now we were seniors and we were one year old in the college. Juniors had joined. I didn't do any ragging on the freshers. I didn't attend the freshers' day function, I entered the hall only at the end.

During the function I got clarity about the thinking ability of humans. During the function our class topper made a speech to the freshers with the force of being our C.R. If successful people say about anything, the audience will listen carefully, but if a failure says something people ignore. But actually we get more information from failures, but we don't notice that. We hang on to winners.

Slowly I was getting the hang of things, and during this time my first year results were announced. 50% of the students had kicked their subjects, so I was not very much worried. I had kicked three subjects. I didn't felt bad, because I know about myself, I didn't study and I didn't attempt well, so there is no exemption for me. But still I felt bad. The next day one of my friends came towards me and asked, "What mama, how many subjects you kicked ra?"

He asked just this single question.

With that question I got the meaning of engineering.

In the intermediate all asked about the marks and percentages, but in B.Tech our mates asked us how many subjects we had failed in. This is the simple difference between B.Tech and intermediate. I got the answer.

From then onwards I was relaxed. And I said three, and I asked him how many subjects you have ra?

His reply was the same, "I also kicked three."

"Good ra," I replied.

My uncle asked about my result; I failed in two subjects, I said.

"Hoo that's it, nothing is goes happen; failing in B.Tech is common, you failed only in two subjects, so you are a good student," he said.

What, I didn't get my uncle's words. It's a strange answer from my uncle. After that I felt a little proud because I had failed in only two subjects, and failing in B.Tech is common.

All were in that mood; all were thinking like that.

In the eighth class my brother said, "Don't look behind yourself, only a few members are there, see how many fellows are ahead of you, you have to beat them and move forward."

But here more fellows were behind and with me, so when compared with them I was a little good also. So now I'm not getting how to take my brother's words.

"According to education motivation also needs to change."

Hanging on to the same dialogue is not wise.

After a month the strength of our class was increased. The diploma students also entered. After completing their course, they wrote eligible test for engineering and they directly joined in the second year.

From this year I learned new habits. I found a special interest. I can't treat it as my goal, I will say it as my dream, just a dream. At least once in life I wish it would happen. This dream made me a little senseless, and by this dream I learned new habits; no, not new habits, bad habits. When we like anything we move without sense. I understood this in this case.

Every day we travelled by the college buses. National highway 44, smooth roads, power steering engines, highly experienced drivers… they drove at 90 to 110 speed on the highways and the journey was of forty kilometers. And my bus driver Naganna was a superb driver. He maintained good speed and the most interesting part in his driving was that he made good cuts on the curves with maximum speed.

"His driving made me senseless, ruthless and breathless."

Every day at the Pamidi point he made this breathless cut.

God damn of his driving.

There was another driver like him. His bus number was 3, and we called him 'Thatha' (grand pa). He was an awesome driver, he should have been a formula one driver. His age was above 65, and he couldn't even walk properly, but when he took his driving seat, then he showed the hell. He drove only on the right side of the road, and he never moved to the left side. No one could catch up with his speed. Even if he started his bus later than the others, he would take his bus ahead of the other buses. He had a confident grip on driving.

These two drivers were my heroes, and watching their driving I fell in love with driving; frankly they made me passionate about driving. And I decided to become a driver, and with this passion I learned smoking also. And this interest went to peaks.

"At least once in my life, at the afternoon time on the national highway, I want to drive a bus, by smoking a cigar," I decided. This the dream I made

This was my dream.

Not only driving, I was inspired to smoke too. Because these two drivers liked lighting cigars.

Two passions propelled me towards smoking – one was these drivers, and the other one was my passion, my dream and my goal is "direction." One of my favorite directors also lit cigars. When I failed in inter I thought quietly about my talents, and then I found my passion. I am interested in something, and that something is "direction." I found my interest in direction. At that time my brother had said, "Wait for four years. First complete your engineering, after that if you are interested in the same passion, then we can think about that."

Because of his words I became a little closer to my passion, and I became a little closer to smoking also, but I never tried it on that time.

One day I found a director's photo, in that he was lighting a cigar while thinking. After I got his name I found that he was the famous director Alfred Hitchcock. This photo impressed me more, and these drivers influenced me more than the other.

"My addictive passion makes me addicted to smoking."

College is the best place to learn good and bad things. Here I got a chance to light cigars; I was a little curious about that, so I learned it here. Lots of fellows had those habits her, so without any fear I too learned. And my first cigar I lighted with a fellow, I will remember this fellow till my death because he is the one who lighted my first cigar and who was the witness for my habit.

In this year, I learned yet another habit; I started drinking. No passion was linked with this. It was just for parties. During my friend's b'day party, for the first time I tasted beer, for the first time I sipped it, just a 10ml of beer. It was not that much good, "but the taste makes us to ask for some more," totally the taste was 'not bad to not good.'

And in the next month there was another b'day party. This time my stamina increased to one glass and at the next party it increased to one bottle. From this time I turned to be a countable piece, if any parties were held, they took a count for me also. Some fellows don't smoke, and some don't drink, but a smoker surely drinks, but a drinker may or may not smoke.

In the learning days my friend lit the cigar and he gave it to me, and then I smoked it. But for beer there was no teacher for me. I learned it myself from experienced persons.

"Easily I get addicted to good and bad, but don't know why this bad habit addicts me."

In this second year lots of things happened. Day by day my class room moved far away from me. I started enjoying, but the only detriment was that I was far from college fights and girls. So I missed a little spiciness in the enjoyment.

A piece of unbelievable nonsense happened to me.

My principal beat me twice during this year. In the first year the class was very near to me, so I didn't get any shortage in attendance. But in the second year enjoyment kicked me out from the class. I started bunking. So many times I bunked classes and it became a regular thing for me, and I was never caught by my principal or by anyone else. But every day is not ours, sometimes our day becomes that of others, it happened to me.

From day to day benches were getting empty and our nonsense was also turning out to be a little more, so lecturers were giving complaints, and some fellows were found on the corridors, some fellows were wishing the lecturers in the canteen instead of in class room. Day by day civil branch was turning to be the noisiest in the college. All were fed up with our nonsense, and this made my principal angry, and he decided to punish us.

Like any normal day, one fine Monday I didn't go to the college. On that day our principal came to our class and took a list of the absentees. He warned the remaining fellows and he went out.

Next day when I came to the college my class mates explained the situation, but I didn't take it to be serious, because in the beginning everyone had spoken about the principal and his strictness, but until now I hadn't seen him angry. So I was calm, but my friends were very serious.

I asked Romantic king about the situation.

He said, "Arey I was also absent yesterday."

"Why ra?" I asked

"I have a reason, so I took holiday yesterday," he replied.

And I asked what the reason was.

He stated his reason.

Ok, nice reason, so he could escape from principal's angry emotion.

Ok, but for me there was no reason, so I wanted to think.

After eating breakfast in the canteen I went to the class room. My fellows said, "Arey why did you come to class ra, principal came to class yesterday, and he gave deadly warning ra."

They were frightening me. I said to myself, let's wait for a while, let's see what's going on. Fifteen minutes after class started, principal entered the class room with the list of absentees. What my fellas said was true. I thought I was going to taste my principals punch. And he called out the names. I was the second person in the list. We were made to stand in a line, and the principal came towards us and started beating us. He didn't ask anything he just started his work. The sounds were resounding, the echo travelling from one end to the other end of the class room. And I was next to him, my pulse rate was increased and I'm sweating. He tore my friend's skin, and showed kung fu panda movie to my friend. Then he came towards me and shouted, "Arey remove your spectacles."

I removed my glasses and stood innocently.

"Why did you take leave yesterday?" He shouted at me.

I didn't get anything to answer, and I didn't know what to say also.

Again he shouted, "What's the reason?"

Principal was in readiness to hit, he took me in his hands. Whether I may give an answer or not I was going to get beatings, so to decrease the punishment, I had to give a better answer.

I mentioned a reason which was the reason Romantic had shared with me in the morning. But he was not ready to accept my answer, he slapped me. I shouted, and again he slapped me. Now this time there was no sound from my mouth, he didn't give me a chance to shout.

It was the first time I saw in a professional college, a principal raising his hands on a graduating student. What a shame and what a pity!

In front of girls, hooo God in front of girls, my principal beat me!

Bull shit.

I didn't know how to digest this situation.

In school I had got beatings in front of girls from teachers and from my head mistress. But at that time I didn't feel bad because I was a kid and for a heavy reason I got that, but now this time, God it was too embarrassing. After this situation girls looked at us with great pity.

It was the most embarrassing situation.

God!

In engineering bunking the classes is a normal and common thing, but beating the students is not at all a common thing. To get beating at this age was too bad, and more over I got it in front of the girls in my class.

What the hell,

God damn,

Shit of this. If I talked about this to anyone, they would laugh and show bloody pity like our class girls. What a shameful experience I had at the age of nineteen for a silly reason!

And next to me was Romantic, and the principal asked him for his reason.

He gave his answer.

Principal went wild because again he was hearing the same answer. So he got very angry. He slapped him. But Romantic was not like me, principal's heavy blow on his cheek made him angry too. He shouted at him and pushed him and he kicked the class and went out. Principal got angry on hearing the same answer, and Romantic got angry because of the heavy blow.

Before Romantic I gave an answer, again Romantic also gave the same answer, by hearing the answer principal got mad.

The sudden surprised reaction from Romantic surprised my principal. We were all startled. We all went into shock. Our civil fellow got angry with the principal! Within minutes the news spread throughout the college. For anything, whether for good or for bad, we take the first step. This I understood better.

After the class one of my friends made a call to his dad and cried, "Dad I don't want this college; here principal is beating dad, no dad, I don't want," he cried through his mobile.

As for me, I felt ashamed; I didn't do anything as Romantic had done, or like my friend. Later I ignored it.

One of my friends said, "I didn't get any beating ra, I just covered it with my hands."

Shit!

This is a worse thing than my worst.

Bloody shit of life.

It was the first time for me but not the last time. The next time I got it on the road.

That was the second time in the same year. We are seniors so bunking is not a crime and it is fun also. So obviously I liked it. And we were in engineering so we had a right to bunk classes, and in that we were seniors so for seniors anything is right. Already I had seen an angry face, so there was no need to fear, and I didn't bother about that. If anyone says don't do something, we do the very same thing, we are students no angry face can stop us. So after this situation also I didn't give any break to bunking.

One day our class mates decided to play cricket. Gooty was just 3 km from college, for parties, movies, for relaxation, to play and for anything we moved to Gooty. So for every action and for every reaction we moved to Gooty. On that day our mates were going to Gooty and I too decided to go with them. Actually I don't play cricket and I don't play any games, even then I decided to go because I like bunking more than playing. And I was not close to some of my friends who spent most of their time in class rooms, and I couldn't spend time in class without noisy fellows.

First all of us went to the canteen and there we divided into groups. Once we divided ourselves into groups, we went from the backside of the college. But what we did was that we didn't run, we just moved casually. While we were moving out of the college, one of my lecturers saw us, but he didn't take it as serious because he thought that just one or two fellows were moving, and so he didn't mind much. But after finding a group of boys missing, he was shocked. But we didn't care much about him. Immediately he mentioned this to our P.E.T sir. We escaped as we were out of the college.

When we were getting on to the road, our principal's car had passed us. Now we were shocked, as one of my friends said, "Arey principal saw us. I don't know whether he saw us or not, but the car has passed, so we have to move from here fast."

We got on to the road and we waited for an auto rickshaw. After a minute an auto came by, we raised our hands to stop it, but the driver didn't stop the auto. We understood that something had happened; we ran behind the auto and got into it. The auto driver said, "Hey kids, your principal is coming; please get out from the auto. He has seen you."

But we didn't bother about his words; we were in a hurry to escape from the principal.

"Anna hurry up anna, go anna go, go anna," we cried!

The auto driver said, "Guys your principal watched us; you can't move far. Let's get out from auto. If he catches hold of us he will scold me also," he cried.

But we didn't listen to his words.

"No anna, go anna, go move fast anna."

Auto driver raised his speed, but already our principal had started his chase on a bike. He was coming like a hunter and we were escaping like innocent deer. If he were to catch up with us, he would surely fry us.

Our principal overtook our auto and stopped. Today we were becoming a good dinner on his plate.

"Get down from auto," he shouted.

One by one we got down from the auto and he fried us on the road. All people on the road were watching us. Quite close to our college there was another engineering college too. The students of that college were also watching us like hungry foxes. All the travelers were watching this fry making process. But I was not noticing this, I was thinking how to escape, but it was not possible. I was caught by the hunter and it was his time, he was in a wild hunger, and I was on his plate. I couldn't jump from his plate and there was no chance to skip. P.E.T sir was standing nearby in readiness to catch anyone who tried to escape. Even if I tried, how far could I go, I had no chance; if I tried, the hunter would mince me into pieces.

"And I had no chance and I was getting ready to sacrifice my shyness on the road."

One after the other, all were being fried.

He pulled me over and bent me, and gave me a heavy blow on my back.

"Ouchhh!" I shouted, and he pushed me on the side of the road.

"Go, go to the class room. Within five minutes I will be there in the class room, if you guys are not in the class then I will show you again," he shouted.

Ooffff!

We ran into the class, took a deep breath and waited for the hunter. I thought principal was hunting for us in another class room. But he didn't come to class.

The first time I had felt shame, but this time I felt worse than ever, and had no words to explain this worst feeling.

I don't know how the remaining fellows took this, but for me this was the worst.

On the road I sacrificed my shyness.

In the same year I had two shameful experiences.

Actually our principal was good, and he was the favorite of the students, the only major defect in him is his anger. If he caught anyone, he didn't try to think; before opening his mouth he raised his hand. Except for that, nothing was bad in him.

In the second year our class room was shifted to the first floor. After lunch we would stand on the corridor and make some funny nonsense on the girls and on ourselves and on everyone. We laughed for meaningless words. More than bunking the classes standing on the corridor and making fun is the best time pass.

I found more fun on corridors.

Bunking classes is quite good and I felt very good while bunking classes. After the first period we moved out and checked where P.E.T sir was. We went to the ground if he was there, then we directly moved to the bathroom, and waited till he went off. After that we moved out. Sometimes I didn't even go to classes. When I stepped out from the bus, I moved straight to the canteen and from there I vanished from college.

In school I was good with malpractices and rewriting in progress card. After school I stopped malpractices. But I'm not averse to nonsense.

Let's move into the story.

If we didn't pay any fees then we didn't get the accountant's sign and seal in the 'no dues' form. If we didn't get accountant's seal in 'no dues' form, then we didn't get application form to apply for the exam. So to apply for the exam we want application form, and for that we had to get 'no dues' form.

In the second year I didn't pay the bus fee, so the accountant didn't put his signature on the 'no dues' form. And I didn't have money to pay. Then I made a plan to steel his rubber stamp. But some fellow had stolen it before me.

God! Even for this there is competition.

After losing his rubber stamp, the accountant was so furious that he was not listening. So asking and requesting him was a waste of time. So I made another plan.

I went to a stamp shop and got a new rubber stamp, which was similar to the one our accountant used. From then onwards I started using this stamp. But later on, after losing the stamp the accountant got another stamp which was quite different from our stamp. But even then I used my old stamp because no one checks the format of seal.

Later I found that the stamp that was lost had been stolen by one of my fellows.

So in this manner my second year also came to an end. In the second year we had two semesters; in the first semester I kicked two subjects, and in the second semester I kicked four subjects out of six subjects. I completed the remaining two subjects only because of my lecturer.

In the first year during the chemistry lab, he had warned me. Later he turned out to be my favorite teacher.

In the first semester I didn't like him, because every time he caught me, and in labs he showed me bloody hell. He was not that strict, but pointing me out every time made me a little angry with him. During the second semester he came close to us. Actually, I don't know whether he changed or we changed him, but in total he had changed a little bit; whatever it may be, he came close to me, and he explained those two subjects. They were very easy subjects but I found them difficult. His explanation showed me that those two subjects were too easy. So I cleared those two subjects under his guidance. And the remaining four I kicked. If he hadn't taken any care, then I would have kicked in those two subjects as well. He is just like my seventh class teacher.

There was another lecturer who scared me a lot. A strict lecturer, he was too strict in class and in labs. He gave good marks on labs, but before giving it he showed cinema. More than the others, roll number 142 experienced this. He watched his movie, he watch the whole movie at lab external. I didn't have much interaction with him because I stayed far away from those strict lecturers. And he was the only lecturer who frightened me.

I was completing my 'supplies' (supplementary exams) a little slowly, and I was failing in subjects a little fast.

In the second year I found a "forbearance" guy.

He was a fantastic 5.

In this year a mild incident happened.

After one and half years I found his amazing attitude.

He was different from the other fellows and he was too good.

He was also like me, but a little faster in kicking subjects.

One fine 'supply' time we got the 'supply' exam notification. All the 'supply' candidates paid their 'supply' fee. But this guy didn't, he waited till the last date because he had paid all his money for the 'supply' exams, and he wanted some more money to pay, but his father put him on hold. He was using his father's total salary only for 'supply' fee. With his 'supply' fee a normal middle class family could survive easily. So it spells his gratitude on supplies.

So on the last day his father sanctioned the money and he gave it to my friend and said, "Arey pay my supply fee."

Then this fellow paid the 'supply' fee.

At the time of the exam, he went to the HOD's room to get his hall ticket. There he did not find his hall ticket, and the HOD asked, "Arey have you paid the fee?"

"Yes sir, I paid," he replied, but he didn't find his hall ticket.

After checking a couple of times he found his hall ticket, and seeing his photo he said, "Sir, this one sir, this is my hall ticket."

Until then he had been checking his hall ticket by searching for his number, but he didn't get it, and at last he got it by seeing his photo.

Seeing the hall ticket number, the HOD said, "Arey this is not yours, it belongs to 140 and you said your number is142."

"Sir its mine sir, look at the photo," he cried.

Then the HOD took the hall ticket and checked carefully. "Don't you know how to fill an application?" He screamed.

Seeing his hall ticket he was shocked.

"Sir I did not fill it up sir. My friend filled the application sir, so instead of my number he wrote his number sir," he said.

Here 140 made a mistake, on the fee payment day he attached the photo and wrote the correct name and everything else correctly, but in the hall ticket block he wrote 140 instead of 142. He didn't notice it and with the wrong number he submitted the application. Now 142 got his hall ticket with his name and with his own photo, but with another hall ticket number.

He asked the HOD about the correction of the number, and then HOD sir said, "Arey there is no chance for you. Already one set of hall ticket numbers are with the university, so now you don't have any chance, and if you write your exam, I don't know how the result will be. Now I can't do anything, before submitting the application you have to check twice. And my opinion is, don't write your exam; you won't get your result, so sit silently."

We don't know how the fate will be, staying calm means losing a chance, so it's better to write the exam than being silent. So he attempted the exam.

But he failed in the exams. I don't know how he wrote, but he had a reason to fail, but he never blamed him. After getting his result, he was quite normal; he didn't take badly about the result. But the miracle was that 140 completed his subjects. In his hall ticket he had his own number and in 142's hall ticket also the same number 140 was there. The same number was there in two hall tickets, but nothing went wrong.

Ram (140) cleared his subjects.

After the whole incident I asked to Ravi (142), "Arey didn't you feel bad about your result?" Then he said, "No need ra, already the mistake has been done; now there is no use in reacting. If I scold him what will be the use ra," he replied.

Just a simple answer was what he gave.

But hearing this, I was shocked.

"He takes the total mistake as a mistake," he didn't take it as serious.

I didn't expect this from others and surely I can say no one answered like him. Even I myself can't think like him.

In the second year I introduced myself to the college and college also introduced herself. But habits, enjoyment are strictly stuck to college. After the college I stuck to home, I didn't go out, I just stayed at home watching serials.

In this year college taught me so many things and new lessons. Habits, enjoyment and all I got in these semesters, except girls. I don't know why I didn't move close with them. But I was interested in girls. My crush again entered my thoughts. Again the fatty angel entered, but this time I didn't see her and didn't know how she looks, and I didn't even try to see her.

In the final months of this academic year, I bought a mobile and I found Facebook on it.

Zuckerberg, the CEO of Facebook.

For lots of guys like us, he made a social network site to catch up with our lost crushes. Don't know how many fellows find their crushes in Facebook, surely every fellow finds, and some fresh fellows also get their crushes from Facebook.

It is like finding our lost moms, finding our lost twin brother, finding our lost shirts, and finding our past memory.

I created an account in Facebook and I found my college mates. I sent a friend request to them. I searched for my school mates, and here I found my fatty angel. I saw her name on Facebook. God, I found her name.

I… I… I found her on Facebook

I screamed.

No words, when I got her name on my slam book I was surprised that time, now again I was out of words on finding her on Facebook.

Don't know how a person reacts when he gets his love, but a person, after a long time when he gets his lost crush, the feeling is inexpressible.

She is using Facebook. I felt so happy seeing her.

When seeing her name on Facebook my past was regenerated in my mind, and I felt the pain of that day when she made me angry. I remembered the past scenes, and my brain recollected the farewell day scene. Reliving this I got an emotional smile on my lips. Lovely days, and lovely farewell day.

Without any further delay, I immediately sent a friend request to her; that was my first friend request, which I sent to my fatty angel. After that I sent requests to all my class mates.

And I checked her details on Facebook, but no use, she didn't mention her number. I got some details about her studies. And I checked her photos but no result. I too never uploaded my photos, then how could these girls do so. No, they never upload photos.

After "four" years I had found her, I didn't know whether she would accept my request or not. And I didn't know whether she remembered me or not. I was waiting.

After some couple of weeks I think, I opened my Facebook, she had accepted my request.

Gooodeesss…,

I got a message from Facebook that,

"NOW YOU ARE FRIENDS WITH (!@#$%^&) FATTY ANGEL."

Seeing this I 'rock and rolled' on the bed.

She had accepted my friend request.

Seeing the message from Facebook, I was out of words, she had accepted my friend request. Double happiness......

I am her class mate so she had accepted my friend request, but for me she was not only a class mate she was much more.

Don't know how I would react if she accepts my proposal, but I reacted more than that now.

But I never made any conversation with her; I was not courageous enough even to message her.

In B.Tech none of the girls in my class had her name. That's why I'm distant with my class mates, I think.

And I had a little doubt whether she was single or was engaged to someone. And didn't know how to find, if she was in relation, then what could I do. If she was in a relation, it was not fair to chat, I thought. But a senseless mistake I made is that, I didn't even try to find out. In Facebook I checked her relation status, but in our place no one mentions their relation status, actually they don't want to publish their relationship on social networks.

So I never made a chat with her.

Whether she have or not don't know, but the thing I love is her acceptance.

She accepted my request.

In the first year I was near to classes and far to bunking, and in the second year it was reversed, I moved far from classes and came very close to bunking. The whole of the second year changed me lot; this year I learned the meaning of engineering. And I got all enjoyable stuff and some habits. And my engineering started from this year.

From semester to semester subjects are kicking me.

From this year onwards I started paying fine for attendance.

In this year I experienced lot of fun, lot of enjoyment.

In the second year I got about studies, engineering is not the place to study, here we learned how to study, every 'supply' changes us a lot, and every 'supply' taught us something. In the first year I wished to study, so I kicked three subjects, but in the second year first semester I wished to enjoy, so I kicked only two subjects. I think this logic is fine.

Ok, good, but in second year second semester my enjoyment went to little peak, so I kicked four subjects. Again I was startled because I was not getting how to handle engineering, and I was not getting how to maintain enjoyment and study in equilibrium.

"But I never felt bad because engineering never makes us feel bad."

2012–2013

THIRD YEAR

From year to year I was getting more and losing also more. In the first year it was just an year, and the second year, it was not an year, it was an year of enjoyment. I enjoyed and I introduced myself to college life, year to year I was changing a little. I found myself in the second year, my passions and new habits, everything I found here. I took my habits and passions to the third year also.

Third year was the most fantastic, fabulous, awesome good year in my life. I don't know how many best things happened in my life or how many best things are going to happen in future. But this was the best fabulous year.

After this year I was totally changed.

My confidence increased in this year, this year made me stand stable.

First year I'm regular to classes and irregular to bunking.

In second year I'm regular to college but not to classes and started bunking.

In this third year I'm regular to bunking and irregular to classes, not only for classes even to college also.

From my intermediate years I hated Saturdays. So from intermediate onwards I started skipping college on Saturdays.

This continued to B.Tech. From first to last year my college never saw me on a Saturday.

In the third year my absence from classes progressed. My attendance decreased slowly. My third started with 50-50 percent of attendance.

My younger sister completed her schooling and entered the intermediate. My mom sent her to the corporate college, which was twelve hours away from my town. She wanted to become a doctor, so she moved too far to get a seat. So she joined in Vijayawada. From the onwards I was in charge of her; I had to pick her up in holidays.

I had to bring her home and take her back to college. This was a duty I had at home, whenever she had holidays I reserved a seat to Vijayawada to get her. From home to Vijayawada and Vijayawada to home.

At first I got bored with travelling. A twelve hours journey did not suit me, but after some days it became simple and good.

I travelled for hundreds of hours, and through this I became interested in travelling. One full night's journey by bus, listening songs, it's an awesome experience. Whenever I travelled, I used my head phones to make my journey good. I became too much addicted to travelling. Whenever she got holidays, I made reservations in bus. We had train facility also, but I never went by trains, and for this my mom scolded me so many times. But more than in train I enjoyed a lot in bus.

This travelling continued, I travelled lots of times in luxury buses. When I got bored in college, immediately I went home. I moved only in luxury buses, one of my friends scolded me every time for my behavior in choosing buses.

There were lots of buses from Gooty to Anantapur, but every time I chose only luxury buses, because so much of fun and enjoyment I found only on luxury buses, so I prefer that, but no idiot could understand the fun in a luxury bus. So every time they scolded me.

Travelling in bus was an awesome experience for me, when I felt free I just travelled. I want to be alone, but without sounds I can't survive; I want to feel loneliness, but without any disturbance I can't enjoy. To feel fresh recipe of loneliness, travelling is the best part.

Hundreds of kilometers and hundreds of hours I travelled to enjoy my loneliness. But every time I was not alone.

We feel that we are alone, but around us we are not. Sitting on the hill and thinking about something is not what is meant by being alone; in our thoughts we are with someone which makes us to think. After our death also we are not alone. We are buried on the previous souls' place, at night time we meet new mates. Even a soul also needs someone that's why they possess someone's body.

"When we feel that we are single, at that minute on that dramatic thought we are single."

To feel the heights of enjoyment I wished to travel with my thoughts.

So I became truly addicted to travelling.

By travelling from Anantapur to Vijayawada, and picking up my sister I got one thing.

If a family has two boys then the responsibilities and works are separated equally, and this happened in my family also.

Responsibilities to elder one,

Works to younger one.

Until now I had stuck to home, moving to general store, getting some groceries, that's it, no extra heavy work. But in this year, my works had changed totally. These works made me a little elder. I was taking care of all the works.

Running from here to there and there to here, taking care of my responsibilities, by this my attendance also went too low.

And in this year another big surprise happened in my life.

This was the biggest surprise in my life.

It was that I kicked my glasses.

This surprise made this year to special.

Many years back, it was nearly ten years ago, a strange friend entered my life, which made me dumb in front of life. I missed all my life because of that. I missed all my fun, my enjoyment and every recipe of my life I missed. My life was like a clove without its tingling taste.

I got spectacles; for the past ten years I had been wearing them. Actually I am reserved, and these glasses made me more reserved and more helpless. While moving to upper classes my sight also got promoted from point to point and the size of the glasses also increased from millimeter to millimeter. And my power increased so high, that at some stage my eyes surrendered to glasses, without glasses I couldn't do anything. I surrendered to my glasses.

I didn't know whether I could ever see this world without glasses or not. At least once I wanted to check this world without glasses, and this was the wish I made every time, and didn't know when this would happen. I cried lots of times. And I broke my glasses lots of times.

"I want to enjoy but by wearing spectacles I can't,

I wish to play but with this I don't.

I wish to run but don't know how many meters I can, wearing this."

"When I look back to recollect my past, I can't even imagine my past without glasses."

My spectacles had a more beautiful past than me. I walked with them, I watched with them, I enjoyed with them and I saw my life with them. Without them my life was blurred.

The last thing I did at the end of the day and the first thing I did at the begging of the day was only one work; that is removing my glasses at night on my bed, and wearing glasses on my bed before opening my eyes. Lots of glasses have changed but the daily routine work did not changed, every day I did the same work.

I was fed up with glasses, and I was waiting to kick them out, but I didn't get the time.

After all the frustration of the past ten years, now this year I finally got the time and chance to get rid of my glasses.

Now I got a chance to kick my glasses and my dreams were coming true. Now I was removing it, I was getting released from glasses and from frustration. Now I could see the world without sticking any object to my eyes.

First Vinod kicked his glasses and from him I also decided to kick it. He was the second person, I was the first one who got glasses. He followed me. And he was the first one to have the surgery, and I was the second one.

After his surgery I talked to my mom about it, and mom posted the news to my brother. He enquired about the laser treatment for sight correction, and he asked Vinod, and enquired with the hospital as well. After the surgery Vinod went to Hyderabad for a regular check up, and with him I also went to get the details of the surgery.

This was the first time I was moving to Hyderabad, and I didn't know how Hyderabad would be. From my childhood onwards, I had been hearing about Hyderabad and its greatness. I had seen Charminar lots of times on TV, and the most interesting part about Hyderabad is that all the film actors are in Hyderabad. I had seen all the actors in films, and I had seen them on TV, so it was a pleasant feeling for me that I was going to that place and my feelings were inexpressible. Only my face could exhibit the feeling better than my words. It was because of my sight that I was going to Hyderabad. This was the only good thing that happened because of my sight.

And another good thing I got through glasses was that actually my looks spell about my attitude, and these spectacles made me blind good and more innocent.

And after all this I was going to undergo surgery at the same hospital where Vinod had. But for me the cost of surgery was a little higher, because my sight needed more correction than Vinod. But we didn't have an option; if we wanted to have the surgery we had to pay, and there was no bargaining also. If not I would still stay with bloody glasses. So my brother and mom made calculations about the importance of surgery and at last they decided.

Ok.

"I get an approval to spend huge amount of money for my enjoyment."

From childhood onwards I was the kid on whom most money was wasted. Unlike my sister and brother, I didn't study in corporate college; I didn't spend money like them. But I wasted more money than them. Just sitting at home, I used up heavy amounts.

And now this one… we paid half of the amount before the surgery. And the surgery date was not yet fixed.

In between that another desirable incident took place. My schoolmates were organizing a get together party,

Yes, it was a desirable party for me; after four years I was getting a chance to see my crush. A couple of months back she accepted my friend request, and now it was a chance to see her. When my friend made a call and spoke about the party, this was the only thought that came to my mind. And the only question I asked him was, "Arey, are girls coming to the party or not."

He said, "Yes mama, they are coming."

"Are all coming," again I asked.

"Yes ra, all are coming to the party," he replied.

So she was also coming to the party, and so I wished to go to the party under any condition.

Now I had a problem; if I got a surgery date on the date of the function, then what should I do, I couldn't escape. But I had to go and I didn't know whether I would get this chance again or not. And I thought about postponing the surgery. But how could I say so to my brother, if I said so, he would just kick me out. What a frustrating time I met, no thinking and no help. Only a miracle could help me this time.

I waited till the last minute.

Yes,

Yes, a miracle helped me.

I didn't get the surgery date, so I can go now, hoo goddess thank you.

It was a great pleasure to meet my class mates.

After long years I'm going to see,

With great happiness I went to my home town to attend the happiness party. I stayed at Vinod's home.

Every time when I went to my home town, I stayed at Vinod's home. On the day of the party Vinod and I went to the school. With great curiosity I went to the school to check on her.

My school, I entered my school… A blessed full blast of fresh air touched my face, there I found my crush wearing jeans and a light colored top walking towards the church, with facing down. Hoo God, no change in her, she had just put on a little more weight. She still looked like a fatty angel. The minute I met my past it seemed to be me to be the present. My past welcomed me.

The function had started, all my mates were coming and wishing each other, but she was not there. Where is she? I was searching for her but I couldn't find her in the function.

I didn't get it. Had she come or had I failed in recognizing her? I didn't get this. Four years back I had first seen her, now she must have changed a little, if I see her at least I can guess that it is she, but I did not find any girl with the same face cut in the party. I wandered through the party, but it was of no use.

God, this was a bad surprise.

My happiness burnt out within minutes. She had skipped the function. With lots of hope I came to the function and I even ignored my surgery. But she was not here.

First time I had scolded her heavily and badly. When I got a beating because of her, I scolded her, but not so heavily. But this time it was heavy scolds.

I came to the get together function only for her, but she was absent from the party. What a worst fate I faced. Four years after leaving this place, I had come here for her, but she was not here. She kicked my happiness.

I ran out to get some oxygen (smoke) with my smoking friends.

I stayed till the last minute. But she didn't come to the function. My body was present, but my mind was absent. I was still searching for her, but she was not. I was curious about her, so I was here, but she was not curious, and I don't know what busy work she had to skip the function.

My mom says that angels and devils can predict anything, but why didn't my fatty angel get my emotion. Was she engaged to someone?

God no!

Lots of questions came to my mind, but I didn't get a single answer. I didn't get how to find her, and I didn't get whom to ask about her. I missed her. I missed a chance to meet her. And I didn't know when I would get a chance like this.

No other chance, I had lost the only chance.

I felt too bad.

"Really without her involvement she is playing with my emotion. Only devils and angels can do this."

At that moody time I found a beautiful. Her nose was pretty attractive. She was my classmate and I didn't remember at which class she had studied with me, but I remembered her name. Not like my fatty angel, but ok, her looks were good enough to kick me out of my moody state.

She stayed just for a minimum time at the function, and after the lunch she ran away. After the function I got her details. I got her name, her college and her Facebook ID. And I sent a friend request to her but till now she hasn't accepted my request.

After she left, again fatty angel stroked my mind.

Good fun in function but I missed the fun in the function.

The party ended with a little fun and with two cigars.

At night I stayed at Vinod's home. And the next day I went to a place where I had never gone earlier, even in dreams, I hadn't thought about that place.

It was the police station.

Srikanth, another of my classmates and I went out on bike. Riding three on a bike in town is wrong. But we are students, we didn't mind any right or wrong, we minded only what our mental brains said, so nothing stopped us. So we moved on our bike. At the bus stand, I again saw yesterday's beautiful. She was waiting for the bus. She was studying at a place outside the district. While I was crossing the bus stop, she also saw me, I think.

On seeing her I said to Srikanth, "Arey Sri, turn back, turn back ra."

"Why ra?" he asked.

"Urgent ra just a small work, turn back once," I cried.

"Arey already we crossed the traffic police ra, if we go again surely he will catch us ra, no ra it's not safe ra," he replied.

But I didn't bother for his words, I cried, "Arey Sri, please ra turn back once ra."

I forced him and what could he do, he turned the bike. And straight to the bus stop we moved. The traffic police were standing there in the middle of the road and counting money. Because of my words Sri moved towards the bus stop, but seeing the traffic police Sri stopped the bike and turned it back, but one of constables watched us and followed. Sri took the bike and parked it aside, and he gave it to my friend and whispered, "Arey you move from here."

But already the mistake had happened. The constable passed near us and asked where the bike was, and Sri said, "Sir, the bike was not ours, it was my friend's. He took it and went away."

But the constable was not satisfied with our words and said, "Our sir is calling, come with me."

Sri and I went with the constable. There the head constable was counting the collected fine and asked where the third person is. Sri was giving answers to his questions and trying to escape from fine. But the constable was already drunk, and he wanted fine to get half kg mutton, so how could he leave us. And Sri is a miser and he never makes his pocket empty. Sri was trying to escape from him without fine and I didn't disturb them. Constable was asking and Sri was answering, and I was playing with mobile.

Sri was tired with answering and took my mobile to make a call to his father. Then immediately the constable took my mobile from Sri and put it in his pocket.

Hoo God,

Shit, now my mobile went into constable's pocket

Oooffff I entered into the conversation.

When we lose our thing it won't come back, from my childhood I have been seeing this. Now I lost my mobile and it was taken by the police. In lots of films I saw that the things that are taken by police never come back.

Until that time I was standing like a proud buffalo and playing with the mobile; now I wanted to shout. I asked for my mobile, but he didn't give it back, and was asking for the third person and our bike.

Again I asked for my mobile but he was not giving and going on asking for bike and third person.

"Where is the bike?"

"Sir it's not here, my friend has already taken it away, so how can we bring it?" I replied.

If I waste time she would leave from there. I wanted to see her. Arguing with him is not a good act.

I lost my patience. "First give me my mobile," I asked.

And he too lost his patience.

He not only shouted, he did more than that. He overacted on the road. He pulled us.

I went to peak and I shouted.

I explained rules and regulations to the drunken police in a louder voice.

"Is this the way a police can behave with students, if we did a mistake then you have to ask for fine, I will pay bloody fine. But you don't have any book and billing slips for fine, so how can we pay fine, all are running in hurry without any license, and you are not checking them, but you guys caught us and are asking for fine. Do you think we are illiterates?"

I shouted like hell, "Taking my mobile is not fair sir. You will pay for that sir," I warned them.

Already he was in a drunken stage; if I do something extra how could he tolerate. If a policeman shouts on the road, it doesn't matter, but if an ordinary fellow shouts at the police, it certainly matters.

"Hoo my son you are looking like my dad, saying rules and regulations to me, come let's have a cup of tea in the station, our Sub Inspector is good at rules and regulations," he replied.

I was also in a fiery mood. "Ya ok, let's move to the station." I shouted. Sri didn't understand anything.

He took us to the station.

This was the first time I was entering a police station. It was not like what I had seen in films, it looked normal. I didn't see any thieves in the station; the station was filled with politicians and street leaders. Yes, from the 19th century till now, no thieves are found in stations, all are leaders fighting for freedom, fighting for the good. In the 19th century we saw freedom fighters. Now we are seeing leaders but the reasons have changed.

We both went to the S.I.'s room. The S.I. was busy with head phones, he was enjoying music. The constable told him about us, and then the S.I. shouted at the constable.

Hoo here constable is dumb so no need to worry, I thought. That S.I. was well known to Sri's father. Sri told him about his father.

The S.I. said, "Leave them," but before that he took a short class for me, because I had quoted some rules and regulations. After that they released us from the station. While going back I took my mobile from the constable. Then he asked me a question.

"Hello boss, what are you thinking about me?"

"No sir nothing, I didn't think much about you, that's why I am here," I replied.

After ten minutes the three of us were released from the station.

I am released from the station.

In eighth class I was tonsured because of a girl,

In ninth I was beaten up by a girl,

Now I went to police station because of a GIRL.

Some link is there between me and girls. That's why I am facing this type of incidents. I think in my previous birth they got something bad from me, so now they are taking revenge.

Because of girls I experienced different things and now it's my crush time; I don't know what I experienced by my crush, already I got a beating because of her. But I didn't throw her away from my thoughts; I still hold her in my mind.

From this incident I experienced a strange surprise.

With this my get together ended, with strange experience and with a disappointment.

Again I didn't see her, I went to the police station because of her curious nose, but I missed her. She ran from Jammalamadugu.

Now my surgery… two months after the get together I got the surgery date. After my surgery I was going to remove my glasses. Thinking of kick out my glasses was the most relieving feeling I experienced. I felt happier than ever. My ten years' inexpressible sadness was going to leave me.

On 16th December I had a surgery to my left eye. In just five minutes the doctors completed the first surgery successfully, and on the next day the next surgery for the second eye was scheduled. They tied up the operated eye with a bandage. Next day I went to hospital to have another surgery. But before that the nurse came and took me to the rest room, and here she removed the bandage covering the eye.

I sat on the chair facing the roof, and slowly the nurse started removing the bandage. Layer by layer the cotton was removed by the nurse. I was eagerly waiting to feel my vision, and she was removing with her sensitive fingers like an egg skull when a chicken is trying to come out from it. My eyelids were fluttering to open. After two minutes she removed the bandage, slowly I opened my eyes. It was a little blurred, I fluttered my eyelids and then I saw a blurred face. My left eye was good and right eye was in blurred vision.

She asked how your vision is, and I said that it was bad. Then she closed my right eye with her hand and asked, "Now how are you feeling?"

I said, "I'm feeling beautiful."

She was surprised at my answer,

Yes, I was feeling beautiful because I was seeing a beautiful face. Goddamn beauty she was, I saw the beautiful face of the nurse, my left eye has damn luck, I can't even try to shutter my eye lid and she was standing in front me and closed my right eye. I was enjoying her beautiful face. What a luck my left eye had. I think she was from Kerala.

She looked tremendous. Her eyes were very attractive. She started cleaning my eye, and I was watching her as she was cleaning.

After that I went to the operation theater to get another surgery for the right eye, and within just five minutes it was also completed. Next day I went to the hospital to remove the bandage to my right eye. I waited for her but this time another Kerala nurse came and removed my bandage. She also looked pretty. But yesterday's beautiful one was a little too good. My two eyes have pretty luck, but the left eye was more blessed with a beautiful nurse. From then onwards all were looking beautiful; even the word untidy was looking very beautiful. The whole earth was looking beautiful to my naked eye.

It was rebirth to my vision.

"I'm feeling the sense of vision."

My friend of ten years left me and went into the cupboard. I had changed a number of glasses during the past ten years and now there was no use for glasses any more. The thought that "I don't use glasses from now on" was making me happy.

What a pleasant moment I had, I didn't even think that I was going to kick my glasses, but now I had removed my glasses, and without them I was seeing the entire world with my naked eye.

After the surgery my brother asked how I was feeling. How could I express my feelings! It was my feeling that I was enjoying, no one can understand another's feeling without any experience. If I were to tell him, he just understands my feeling, but he can't feel that, so it's better to enjoy it by myself. I didn't give any reply to him. I just laughed.

Even now I don't know how to run, but I want to run

I tried to enjoy but by wearing spectacles I didn't do so,

"When I'm using glasses, I'm not good in games."

"When I'm using it, I'm not good in adventures."

"When I'm using it, I'm not good in enjoying."

"When I'm using it, I'm not good in sleeping also."

From now

"Even though I'm not good in games, but now I can play."

"Even if I am not good in adventure, but now I can move."

"Even if I am not good in enjoying, but now I can do."

"I am not good in sleeping but now I can."

The surgery increased my confidence.

Now I am alright, I can and I do.

Lots of fellows are wearing glasses, but I don't know how many guys are feeling its weight on their eyes, but for me it was like hell. I lost my enjoyment and my school days because of it. When I was released from the glasses I felt that I was the happiest person in enjoyment.

A little thing also makes us dull, in my life also it happened, I bent for spectacles and in return I got unsatisfied days.

When I saw myself in the mirror I was looking like a new born baby. I was born like as normal kid with normal parts, but after that I got glasses to my eyes, and after a long time now I was looking like a new born baby.

Ok I am free now, I can see all. And my remaining days are going to be good. Every time my brother says, "Now you are looking confident ra. After surgery your attitude has changed ra."

Yes my attitude changed after the surgery. I too wished for that.

My happiness was regenerated.

My days without glasses had started.

Fifteen days after my surgery I went to the college. All my mates asked about my glasses and were shocked at the expenditure. Some of my fellows asked, "Arey was it necessary ra."

Yes for me, because I saw the pain. They don't know what I lost; I know, so no explanation need be given to them.

Before my surgery our third year first semester exams were completed and with that I wrote 'supplies' also and awaited the results.

I saw my first movie on theater without glasses, an amazing experience for me. When I was in school I saw a "spy kid's 3d" movie wearing 3-d glasses over my glasses. That time I didn't feel the experience. If I removed my glasses I couldn't see the movie, so I wore both glasses one over the other, and I missed the thrilling experience. But now I am looking without any weight on my nose. From then onwards I have been doing everything without glasses

Two months after my surgery my college conducted an educational tour. Every year a tour was arranged only for the third years. It was a tour lasting seven days. It was the first time I was spending seven days with my friends. Our batch enjoyed a lot. And for me it was my first tour after regenerating my vision. I wished to blast the days of my tour.

During the tour I learned how to enjoy drinking. Drinking a bottle of beer and shouting after that, and vomiting is not the enjoyment. We have to sip every drop of beer. Without a perfect partner we can't enjoy its taste. After two years I met a perfect partner.

"Naveen"

He calls me Diku. Diku is my nick name in B.Tech. He was the one who gave me this name.

I liked enjoying beer with him.

From the first day onwards we started enjoying. It went to a high on the third day. On the third day we stayed in Kerala. In Kerala alcohol was not sold to minors. They maintain systematic rules. No one spoils the rules. If you want to spoil your life then you have to wait till you turn to a major.

In the night our bus cleaner brought us a box of beer. We were in Kerala, and it was the foggy season, so at night time beer is the best sleeping partner for us.

I hadn't tasted Kerala food till now. It was the first time that I was tasting potato chips, which were roasted in coconut oil. The taste was not good. In our part of the country we use coconut oil for hair, but here coconut oil was used to cook food and for hair as well. Its taste was a little different, not to say bad, it was ok. Actually we use it for munching so at that time no one bothered about taste. Whatever may be the taste, we wanted to eat something, first we needed some stuff to munch that's all.

My stamina was only up to one bottle of beer, it was more than enough for me. But I never enjoyed its taste earlier, whereas here I fully enjoyed its taste. For the first time I enjoyed drinking because of my partner. To make a party, chilled beer and a fine munching is not enough. Along with that we need a fine partner to enjoy, only then can we enjoy its taste.

Before this I had drunk with him, but this time he made drinking too beautiful and enjoyable. Beer was not to taste but to enjoy with friends. Its taste is awesome we can drink two bottles and sometimes it increases to three and even more also. After it kicks the brain then the whole fun starts.

He took two beers and me one and other mate also had as per our ability. After having dinner we fell on the roads. And we started teasing travelers; in the dark night we lit a light with a handful of cigars. We shouted like no others, and this fellow was doing more and more nonsense. When we drink beer we know what we are talking and doing, we are in conscious mind. But excess of beer encourages us to do more action. It intended him to do more. While he drank, his words and his snake dance went to peaks; every action of his was awesome and funny. That night I enjoyed with him a lot. We enjoyed every drop of beer with friends; however the fun may be, but we enjoyed.

"We enjoy every nonsense without sense, only with friends."

"What I enjoyed with him is not a bottle full bear it's a bottle full of fun."

Don't know in future how much I can enjoy beer, but every time while drinking I remember those days.

It was not only the systematic rule that I liked in Kerala. I like beautiful eyes. In Kerala I saw beautiful eyes. Every woman in Kerala has beautiful eyes. Their eyes are more attractive, they draw others looks to them. I saw more and more beautiful eyes. Seeing those beautiful eyes, I and friend decided to do M.Tech in Kerala.

Our tour was turning to little more fun. Day by day percentage of fun was increasing. At the start I thought, "How can I enjoy 7 days," but now I am not counting days.

Every day was a special day for me. Daily we ate three times, morning tiffen, afternoon lunch and at night dinner from a single plate with four to five hands. At the college canteen we ate like this; I learned this in college. When I was a kid my mom had also done the same thing. In a single plate she would keep small lumps of rice for all of us. We did the same as we do in college, numbers of hands in a single plate. After home we feel school and college as our second home. And our friends are our family members. What we do at home we do the same in college. We did the same during tour, one fellow brought a plate full of rice and we all fell on that plate, after it was completed we fell on another plate. Don't know how much we ate, we ate till all plates were empty, and then we washed our hands.

Every day was turning to past. Six days I enjoyed lot. On the last day a strange accident happened. Again I went to the police station, now this time with my friends in another state.

On the last day we went to a place which was 7,200 feet above sea level. The total place is located in hills and mountains. And it is a Ghats road section. All of us went in local buses to view the place. On every curve we found beautiful scenery. Our buses were stopped at one of the scenery. It was a valley. To see that place we had to take tickets, we didn't know that. Some take ticket and some take after the security stops.

But one of my friends is a ferocious one who belongs to another branch; he moved without ticket, and the security guard stopped him. Security guard was an old man but too strong. He looked like an old Kabbadi coach. He was stopping ten to twelve members at a time. When he was stopped, my friend got angry with him and started fighting. It went to a high level and they started beating each other. One of the local men who was selling toys came with a stick and hit my friend on his head. Blood flowed from his head like lava and the fighting went all wrong. And we guys also pushed into the fight. I went in between them to stop the fight. I stopped my friend and I pushed the old man aside; the old man got angry and hit me on my neck with the bark of a tree.

"Mummy," I shouted.

Damn with stopping yaar, that's why I didn't move in between fighting.

I went aside and started rubbing my neck.

God!

This old man was so much more ferocious than my friend.

This was the first time I went into a fight and I got beating. And the fight was going on between the students and security guards. Some of the vendors who work there also came and joined the fight. They were supporting the guards and they were coming with sticks. God! It was becoming serious. I ran from there. Some of the policemen were taking our photos.

What damn thing is going on here, I was not getting.

After fifteen minutes the fight had stopped and now my fellows blocked the road and were saying "Down, down."

"Security guard down down, security guard down down."

What yaar what were these guys doing.

Kilometers of vehicles were stopped on the Ghats road. And tourists also got irritated because of us. And it was not going down, already it had gone all wrong.

And my mates took bamboo sticks to face them and some took stones. Nothing was happening more than that, some fellows were shouting as they liked. My partner heard about me and he took a brick and ran from one end to the other end of the road shouting are you going to taste my punch.

Hoo God,

As time passed, the irritation of the tourists grew worse, and now they started. What I think happened was like this:

Yes, it went wrong now with the tourists, they got irritated and started fighting with us; one of the tourists aimed a blow and my sir had to take it. He bent down and started crying. At last the fight between the security guards and us ended, and now it started with the tourists.

There was no mistake on the part of tourists because they had come here to enjoy… In these busy days getting a holiday and spending some time with family is a tough job. If someone does like this, what could they do? So they also got into the fight.

Some were making calls to news channels. But there was no reply.

I was tired of this. Some of the fellows went into the bushes to get some oxygen. I also went to get some relaxation with a cigar.

After hours the police came and tried to convince us, but it was not going to happen. Our lecturers were not ready to compromise. They took us to the police station. All of us went to the station. Before we arrived, the old security man and some other shop keepers had already gone to the station. I don't know what they had said, but something had happened, and all of them belonged to the same place. So nothing good happened to us, we were just trying.

There I saw a police chief who was not looking like a police at all, his dress sense and his behavior was trend setting and he had a trendy stature. I never saw an officer like that.

He sat on a Jeep and started giving lecture. No violence happened in the station, just two compromising words. That's it.

We left from there, and on the last day no fun happened.

Six days I enjoyed a lot, and on the last day I enjoyed a little more. It was the best surprise gift for me in the tour.

From the tour I learned something.

When I was in sixth, my friends Vinod and Ravi got into a fight for a pen. In front of my house both fellows were fighting. They were quarreling like two cats over a rat. I was enjoying the fight, but after a while my dad came out and saw them fighting, and he got angry on seeing me. I was not doing anything, I was just leaning on the wall and enjoying the show. My dad hit me on my head and shouted at them.

"Idiot what are you doing, here your friends are fighting, but you are standing like a rock. Are you enjoying the fight?" Dad shouted.

I just shook my head.

"Idiot," again my dad shouted.

"If you find anybody fighting, go between them and make them feel like good friends. Don't behave like this," my dad shouted at me.

But now I had entered in between to stop the fight, but all I got was some heavy stuff on my neck. Every time I am getting bad signals from elders.

What we listen to in childhood is good, but applying it on every occasion is bad.

Here stopping the fight was not good material. Getting into fight was the better one.

Between friends it is safe and I have to do as my dad said, but not with outsiders. We have to jump into fighting, that's it. This is the best way, trying to stop is not good in that you also get some blows.

So two options we have, if you can, then jump into the fight; if not just go away from there that is the better option.

"At the kinder garden age I was dependent in reaction. But now I am independent in reaction." According to the situation I have to react. First I have to learn that.

From year to year lots had changed, but in studies nothing had changed.

And about my semester subjects… in the 1st semester I failed in two subjects and in 2nd semester in three subjects.

This went on.

Slowly I started completing my previous years' 'supplies.' And I completed the third year 1st semester 'supplies' at a time. Now I had five subjects pending.

My third year ended with so many memories. In this year a lot happened in my life, a lot had changed, my dreams came true. No it was not just a year, it was a remarkable year from 2012 June to 2013. This year has a golden place in my past.

"In this year 'change' blessed me."

And it was a confident semester for me.

From here 'me' changed to I.

Here I concluded one thing that, how a person get fear by other.

For my surgery I moved from Anantapur to Hyderabad and Hyderabad to Anantapur. First time I went with Vinod for checking. There in Hyderabad, Vinod and I went to my friend's college to meet him in the evening. He came out and he gave us a warm welcome. We both went with him into the college and stayed with him at night in his hostel. All in the hostel were such scared fellows. They were all afraid of the warden. When he spoke about their warden I didn't get any fear or anything, Ya I agreed because I did not belong to this college. So I was not feeling any fear but this fellow was so scared. I laughed at him. "Arey you don't know about him, he is like the head of the hostel."

I imagined my school days, that time how he was, and now how he was. He had changed a little; here he was, afraid of his warden.

From the time we arrived, he was talking about his warden; in the school he was a rebel, but here he was not. He was worrying about a warden. In school he showed hell to all teachers. But here because of a warden he was getting tense.

I concluded one thing. If everyone talks big about a person, eventually we get some fear, and we move far from him. And all of us get disturbed. This had happened in this case. So that's why, he also getting tense. But not for long, someone will arrive to break the silence.

My third year ended with a tremendous surprise.

2013–2014

FINAL YEAR

Last year.
Last year of college,
Last year for bunking,
Last year for nonsense,
Last year for enjoyment,
Last year for scolding's,
Last year for college fighting's,
Last year for beatings from principal,
Last year for studying,
Last year for teasing,
Last year for exams
Last year for graduation,
And last year for everything

But not the last year for 'supplies'. If I didn't complete within this year then I would have to shut my head in front of shame.

Until now I had a final year to look forward to, now I was in final year, and there were no more years to think of. This was my last final year of graduation. So studying and completing 'supplies' was the only weapon to stand up and face every one. If not, my 4 years B.Tech would turn to 5 years.

When I entered the final year I had five 'supplies' on my hands. At any cost I wanted to complete them, and along with this 'supplies' I had the final year's regular subjects also. I had to attempt five 'supplies' and ten subjects of the two semesters. I had to complete all these subjects.

You know what we get after B.Tech, it is only our 'supplies'; fun, enjoyment, bunking, everything stick to the class room benches, nothing comes with us. All that we get in engineering just turns to past and stays in memories, only 'supplies' stay with us. 'Supplies' are our prestige. If we move out of the college with 'supplies' nothing respects you; even your shadow and your face in the mirror also spit on you. So I decided to complete.

In the final year I was the worst student in attendance, only in rare conditions I went to the college. On that time my principal made a rule. It was that, "Every student has to attend the college, if not he will be detained." This rule was made by my principal. Everyone needs 60% of attendance. Year by year we were getting promoted as seniors and year by year our attendance was also counting down. Now we were at the final year, and we were the senior most students, and there were no seniors ahead of us. So who was there to follow the rules? In college we were the ruler breakers.

Every student breaks the rule, no one listens to the rules what do we have to do with rules? Breaking rules is our right and making the rules is the principal's right. Without rule maker and without rule breaker, there will be no college.

I had only 10% attendance by seeing my percentage my teaching staff made a call to my mom, but my brother took the call and listened softly.

After I returned home my brother told me about the call, I didn't know how he reacted to my attendance, but he didn't question me.

Not only in subjects, I was poor in attendance also.

If I went to college I stayed out of the class room or I ran on corridors. Not only me, all my mates stayed on the corridors, no one liked classes. And my lecturers too didn't like lecturing to empty benches so they also started hating class rooms and started staying in the staff rooms.

Class room is a place to make sound and corridor is a place to make nonsense. If we saw anyone coming we moved to the class room and it was a best hiding place for nonsense. In the class room no lecturer can find where the sound comes from. And in corridor no student can find who is making nonsense. Class room is like a mother for nonsense and corridor is like a father for nonsense. Both keep us in concealment.

In this final year again I got a blow from my principal. But this time it was in class room for a shame full reason.

One fine day in the morning time, the principal entered our class room. After a long time he was coming to our class. On that bloody day I was also in the class. And from third year onwards I had started going to college without books. And now also I was a free handed guy. We were standing on the corridor when we heard that the principal was coming. We ran into class and settled on the benches, but I didn't have a single book, and some of the other fellows also didn't have books. I sat on the third bench but my friend called me to the first bench.

I refused to go.

But he forced me, and having no chance I went to the first bench.

Soon the principal entered the class room and he came direct to the first bench.

We all stood at our places. He asked about the strength of the class, and didn't get a good answer. He looked at us and he came towards me and asked about the books. I didn't have any book in my hands, and so was my friend too.

He didn't shout at us, he asked about the subjects.

My friend answered, and now principal asked about the syllabus.

And he was bowled. .

Same situation as what Mr. 142 faced once earlier, he didn't even say the subjects' names and he got his share at that time. Now the principal asked the same question, but my fellow was out. And now he asked the question to me, he asked the chapters in the subjects.

I am clean bowled…

"Sir, first chapter is, is, is, is…" I murmured.

I didn't even know the subject names, then how could I know the chapters. But he didn't ask about the subjects, so I escaped from that. Knowing the subjects' names is the primary thing, if we don't know the subject name what will we do in exams.

But not so far

Still I didn't give an answer to his question.

Again he asked, and again I murmured.

He beat me on my shoulder, "Idiot, don't you know even your chapters."

Again he asked the same question to my fellow, he also didn't know. Subjects were six in number, a little easy to remember, but chapters are not. Who can give answer?

They don't know this small thing also. Every time they shout at us. We are not in school to fight with text books. But they didn't understand.

This was the last time I got a beating. After that I never saw his angry face. And it was the final year for beating also.

First time after three years I fell in studies. In the first year I was near to classes but not to subjects. Now I came nearer to studies. To stand in front of parents only two legs are enough, but before shame I needed some more; I wanted a precious degree also?

So for that I wanted to make some space. I started trying for that.

But I had to cope with heavy 'supplies'. Our super seniors had a fair deal; they could get the graduation degree even after leaving two subjects. But from my seniors onwards, this relaxation was removed. We were all shocked, our seniors fought with the university and they brought the rule back.

So we were happy, and I, I was so happy to get a chance to leave two subjects. Until now I had been thinking that I had to complete the whole degree without any fail. But my seniors brought the rule back. After getting this good news I was happy and I got hope.

University gave a chance to us. . I was so happy to hear that. So many fellows like me were feeling very happy with that rule. Now I could leave two subjects. In five 'supplies' I could leave two, hoo God great deal I have.

But our happiness was not too far gone. From this year onwards another rule was passed. From now jumbling system was introduced by the university.

Shit.

Until now we were writing our exams in our college but from now we had to move to another college. Even having our lecturers and our friends around us, it was getting tough to complete the subjects, but now in another college, where we didn't know the lecturers and didn't know how the college would be. In that critical condition how could we complete our subjects? I saw fewer possibilities for that.

Bad follows the good. If we get a good thing, immediately a bad thing stands in Q to catch up. No excuses.

There were only two colleges near Gooty, one was ours and the other was Gates. So our students wrote in Gates College and they wrote in our college. Just an inter change.

We have to put in our complete efforts; there was no scope for any other extra activities. Gates College was strict. If we didn't take ID cards with us, even the watchman would push us out of the gate.

In the 1st semester I wrote my exams in my college, but even then I kicked two subjects, and I completed two supplies. Still I was in suspense whether I could or not. I was losing hopes, and every time I was trying but again and again the subjects were kicking me far.

Now there was no option for me; I had five 'supplies' and 4 second semester subjects in that I have to clear seven subjects. And only one chance for supplies and we had another extra chance for 2nd semester. After the second semester immediately we have an advance supply. If I kicked in 2nd semester immediately I would get a chance in the advance supply, so in that I have to complete. But surely I have to complete in that. From first year onwards a strange thing was happening to me. If I wrote two 'supplies', that means two subjects, I could not complete them in a single attempt. It was taking two attempts, for every single attempt only a single subject was getting out and another attempt was required for another subject. And I made a calculation and was getting good result. I thought I could complete with this semester.

LAST SEMESTER

4–2, last semester in college. And last semester in engineering.

Project, viva, records and four subjects, that's it.

And no college for us; during the last semester the major time was taken for project.

Project is the only major work we have to do in the final semester. I felt a little tense about project, because here I have to attend for viva also. Viva would be like a personal interview. From the university a fully loaded efficient lecturer would come to our college to know about our projects. And he would ask questions too, and I was not getting it how to face it. Along with the project we had to make a PPT (paper presentation) also, and this had to be done before the project,

So at first I did a PPT on something. I collected all the stuff from internet and I stuck it on the papers. And I presented my PPT.

While giving PPT, for the first time I scolded myself for bunking in engineering. We had English lab in the third year but I never attended it. In the lab we get information about communication, how to deal with an interview and how to overcome in interviews. We get all the communication skills in this lab but I never went for even a single period. While giving PPT I understood this. In engineering bunking classes is important, it's an enjoyable life, but after the engineering, getting a job is more important; it's the life. Life of survival… I understood this in the last days of my college. To fight with survival, communication skills are more important. Lack of communications so many are running on roads.

I completed my PPT.

And now the next was project. My PPT was not good but it will be ok with them. But I had to do big in the project. But my seniors and my mates said, "Arey no need to worry about project it will be ok."

Nothing will happen college will take care of that. All said like this.

Within the time our project had started, but before that there was a batch selection.

So batches were divided. I was in Aza's batch. We were six in that batch, guys in our batch were all funny fellows and all were fellows. And our project was on water supply to rural areas. Aza was our team leader. He was the one who picked up the project. During the project time I got chicken pox.

I skipped from the project but not from the team. I didn't even attend a single day. My fellows did all that was needed for the project. After a month our project was completed, and it was time to record the work. This was also done by my fellows.

After the project we had a net practice. At the net practice time we had viva for all the batches. Our lecturers conducted this viva.

When our turn came up, all six of us sat before the lectures, and they started (viva) asking questions about our project. One of the lecturers asked me; I didn't know anything about the project. And I had a reason, but saying a reason like a kid is not correct, because like my mates, at least I should have referred the book and I should have noted down some important information about the project. But I didn't do anything, I had just come with my record.

Ma'am asked question, to me

I don't know what to say

Hello, say your answer, ma'am again asked. What are you thinking?

I want to escape from this so I have to say something.

Ma'am can I say in Telugu, I replied.

Ma'am was shocked, what hero, what are you saying?

You want to give answer in Telugu. We are not coming in at the final stage. If you give answer like this, you will be kicked out from exam. Ma'am shouted.

Before that first learn some English, ma'am said.

Ok ma'am, I replied.

All my fellows laughed at me,

Stupid fellows.

And the day arrived. Before the day I bought a pair of dress and shoes to present myself well. Because impression is the first and best way to fall on someone's eyes from 7th class onwards I'm hearing this.

I came with a neat and tidy look, but one of my friends came with slippers, I was shocked to see him in slippers… Because, I bought a new dress for this viva, and really I thought about my project viva while doing so. This fellow uses shoes on normal days but now he had come in slippers.

Some fellows came with neat and tidy looks, and some came with casual looks. And I stopped thinking about looks.

Ok whatever it may be, we submitted our records and we sat in the conference hall before the lecturer. She came from the university not from some other local college.

Before it started we had heard about the lecturer, we heard that the lecture was going to be a 'she' and not a 'he.'

Hoo God. They are a little tough to convince. But our lecturers said nothing to worry she is good. First batch went in and they came out happy, but the second batch was not fully happy and so also the third.

Now it's our turn she started asking questions one by one from our project and from subjects also. I got one question and for that I gave half the answer. After that I didn't get another question. After ten minutes we came out from the conference room. We were happy that nothing happened wrong, nothing happened to all batches also. One lecturer came and said, "Nothing to worry guys, you all got good marks in viva."

It was good and great to listen. We all got good marks.

Happily we completed our viva and our college. With this viva we completed our college life, and just a partial enjoy was left. It was the farewell party.

At the afternoon we started celebrating.

"And it was our last nonsense in the college."

We started sprinkling colors on one other. Each and every fellow was sprinkling colors, each and every fellow attended this nonsense for the first time. For the first time I was seeing all the fellows. For the past four years at least ten to fifteen were found to be absent every day and there was even an absentee for the exam. But now there was not even one absent.

Everyone had applied make up with different colors. Our last nonsense had turned into a colorful nonsense and girls also participated in this nonsense. What a colorful thing it was to see. Some changed to black and some changed to red and some were totally colorful. Everyone gave a colorful paw print on the back of everyone else's dress, this paw being a symbol of our memories and our fun.

From here there were no monkey sounds on the college walls, no capsicum rice in canteen, no teasing on corridors, no cries in class room, no beer on friends b'day's, no smoking in Dhaba, no bunking, no shortage of attendance, and we never hear principal's scolding's and no nothing after this day, and this day was last.

On the colorful last day, no past memory turned around me, only happiness of the joy I enjoyed with all the fellows.

Last day I was enjoying in the college, faces with colors speak of our joyful days and the affection between us and with the college.

In the college we can see so many silly fighting, and along with that silly fighting distance also increased between us. But by God's grace nothing of that sort happened to me.

"Everything will be turned to past after this day."

"I am missing all my past."

"I am missing all fifty acres clean ground."

"I am missing my joy and my principal."

"I am missing my college."

In the evening I went home in colorful dress. In the morning I had gone with black bottom and clean blue shirt, but by evening black remained as black, but blue had turned to different colors.

Mom was surprised and shouted at me.

"Ma! It's all fun, see my shirt, how beautiful it is! My friends made it colorful and beautiful with their affection for me."

And I warned, "Ma don't wash it, please keep it safe."

"Idiot," she started scolding, "New shirt, yesterday you bought it, and today you have made it filthy, how can I wash it?"

And my hands went to bed, mom shouted.

"Ma, don't try to wash it, place it safe," I cried.

But moms never take our words, so I wished to place it safe.

"The only thing I get from college is my enjoyable memory and this filthy colorful blue shirt."

And the only part remaining was my final exams and fare well party.

I missed something…

In this year I had fallen in crush. I forgot to say about her, a beautiful crush. After a long time, I had fallen in crush.

She was two years older to me. She also travelled on the same bus. She was not studying engineering. She was doing some other post graduation course in our college. When I was in second year she joined PG in our college.

She looked very beautiful, five feet tall, and her color was a mixture of pale red and yellow, if we slap on her cheeks it would turn to red, her hair was not long and not short, medium hair, very beautiful curly hair she had, when she sat at the window seat her hair flew out from the window like waves in the ocean, and in red dress she looked amazing, red color suited her, red looks very beautiful only when she wore it. And she wore green nail polish, it looked awesome on her feet and I fell in love with green after seeing nail polish on her toes. And her walking style was very innocent. Wearing a bag on her back, her slow and steady walk looked very beautiful to see.

Totally she was a mixture of short height, curly hair, a face colored a mixture of red and yellow, a simple smile on her lips, and her dress sense was very very decent, including her nail polish.

She was very beautiful because she was short,

She was very beautiful because she had curly hair,

She was very beautiful because she had a beautiful color,

She has beautiful legs when she has green nail polish on.

Everything in her was beautiful. I think God took a special interest in her, that's why she was that much beautiful.

From the second year to final she travelled with us in the same bus. From second year onwards I was watching her but I never fell into crush. From the time of her joining onwards she was getting proposals, but she was not reacting. As for me, at the end of college I fell in crush with her. It happened during the time of the exams.

At the exam time I never tried to study while travelling. All my fellows read while on the bus, but for me it was not easy. If I looked at books in bus, I would get a book stroke and my eyes would drop down in sleep. So I didn't read on the bus; instead I tried to take a little rest. From first to last I had been doing this. But this time something had happen. .

My exams had started. For the first exam I sat on my usual place on the bus, I took the book out of my bag, but after five minutes I got book stroke and I closed it. It was a journey of forty-five minutes, and all were busy with books, and I was the single one on the bus without books. I was getting bored; I didn't get anything. I was at the window seat, and my eyes were looking for something. I was in a little chirpy mood. She was five seats away from me and opposite to me. Casually I looked at all the faces; all were busy, and my eyes stuck at her. I saw her, she was looking little blue on white dress, don't know why she was looking like that, I think it must be because of my chirpy mood.

Hoo hooo hoooo she was looking amazing! For the past three years I had been watching her but now she was a looking little crispy. I was seeing her, seeing her, seeing her, ten minutes had passed, and I was not getting bored and no worry of exam bothered me. I was just seeing her.

What damn feeling it is?

It was an awesome feeling. At the time of fatty angel I didn't know the meaning of this feeling, but I enjoyed that time. Now I knew the spelling and meaning, and I was enjoying it also.

And I remembered my fatty angel. I fell in crush with her in the 9th class. It was not a good, enjoyable and understanding time, but still I fell in.

Now in college, at last supper time I fell in crush. No pet names for her, and my brain is not able to find any name, my brain is just capturing her beauty.

And with this thought we arrived at college.

God, I have exam, I forgot about the exam, I didn't study for the exam. Girls make everything to dumb. Without our intention they capture our time, they capture everything. This can be done only by girls. Girls alone can do this.

I really don't know how I wrote the exam. After the exam I came out I started searching for her. I found her on the bus. She sat at the same place. I took a place opposite to her, I was thinking why she was looking so beautiful. Was it that there was something wrong with my eyes? Don't know.

For the next exam I studied at home, I decided not to open book in the bus.

And at the next bus stop she got into the bus, she sat at the same place opposite to me. I started seeing and thinking why she looked beautiful. But I was not getting the reason. I was enjoying it. This continued for the next exam and the next exam. This went on till all the exams ended. All this happened at the time of the 1st semester of the final year.

And we got holidays thereafter. But I didn't have holidays as I had 'supplies'. I knew that she didn't have any supplies even I wandered looking for her.

After the 'supply' exams also I went to college in search of her, and seeing this, my friend Bharath asked me, "Arey you don't come to college even if you have work; but now you came to college what's the reason?"

He asked.

"No ra, I just came casually," I replied.

My total attendance percentage was nearly 50 to 60. I never went to college but now I was going to the college because of her even when we had holidays.

I wandered looking for her like a mad dog.

One fine evening, the college bus was overloaded with students, and some of the fellows like me stood on the footsteps. After forty-five minutes we reached our town and at every stop one by one were getting down. After two stops I got a seat in front of her. In our bus at the door steps two seats are opposite to each other, every time she sat at that place and that seat was opposite to every seat, so every time she was opposite to me. My lecturer got down from the bus at his stop, so the seat was empty, and I was very close to that seat. I ran and I sat there, just two feet away from her. I was very close to her. I had never seen her with this close. I was amazed.

God. She was too beautiful to see,

First time I was seeing her, this close just two feet away.

She wore a maroon red colored dress and she had green nail polish on her left hand; it was looking very, very beautiful. I couldn't see her face to face, so I bent my head and I saw her legs, and the green nail polish to her toe.

Hoo God, what happened to this green, it is looking good.

Bloody damn, green also looks beautiful, no she made it beautiful, only girls make everything so beautiful and they make every untidy thing beautiful. Every untidy face turns to neat and clean. If girls stick to home then the entire tidiness will turn untidy. No fellow will use creams, no fellow will follow dress sense, and no fellow will be stylish.

If there is no girl "a fellow will be like a fellow."

Girls are beautiful, so they make everything too beautiful, but boys are not, so they turn to beautiful.

Seeing the green nail polish, I fell in love with green color. And it became a favorite color to me.

And next day with the next color, all colors were being turned beautiful by her.

But it was not a long lasting crush.

The 2nd semester started and now I neglected her, due to project work I became busy. Only occasionally I went to college. And she too was in final year, so she also had project work and she turned to be irregular.

During the second semester I saw her only four to five times.

Fine and beautiful crush.

This was a more beautiful crush than the earlier crushes.

-|-|-|-

And after all this I wrote my final exams. These were my final exams in B.Tech. And thereafter I never wrote exams. My graduation was getting completed with these exams. From the time I wrote my first exam I never felt any emotion, I was not frightened about the result, but now I was a little nervous because this was my last exam. 'Supplies' are secondary but this was last exam with all my mates.

My exams were completed.

After the exams we held a farewell party.

At the function our principal gave a speech about us.

He shared his inner feelings with us.

"You are the worst and the best batch. For anything good and for anything bad you guys will be at the forefront. For nonsense you are in front, for college fights you guys stand first and for study you guys take the lead." These words my principal used.

"Yes we are the rascals of the college."

For everything we stand in front line even in good and bad.

Some of our lecturers praised us and gave advices about the future.

We took selfies with our dear ones, with our guides. And I took our class mates autographs on my T-shirt.

In the afternoon we had a delicious meal with our class mates. Last meal with my mates. In the canteen we shared lots of plates, lots of hands in single plates. This is our last meal with my mates.

After we went to our class room, one by one started sharing their feelings of their past time.

And I cried on the stage. I went on to the stage to share my feelings, but my words were defeated by my tears. I cried. When I was beaten up by my principal on the road, I didn't feel any emotion, but now my tears were not stopping. When I got those tears I understood what I had lost. I was missing lots of fun. No, I missed lots of fun.

With me some of the other fellows also cried on the stage.

For four years we ran with each other, we fought and we shook hands after it was over. We found some fun even when we fought. And now the present went off, and now it turned to past.

Days gone and the happiness also went with past.

Enjoyed a lot this last day.

From tomorrow onwards I needn't go to college, I will stay at home, this thought made me cry.

At night, for the last time we had a party. I sat on the floor and I started recollecting my days. My friends brought beers, for the first time I sipped only half a bottle of beer and the remaining I gave to my partner. He made chicken curry. It was tasty, and I ate that with some sorrow.

"With wet eyes I smoked a packet of cigars."

My total percentage of happiness was just fifty to sixty percent. If I went some more days to college without 'absentees' I would have got some more percentage of happiness. I lost 40% of the enjoyment. But every minute, every second I enjoyed with them. I didn't get into fighting and nonsense like my fellows, but every time I ran with them, I laughed with them. If any verbal fighting took place, I would be in that, I even got angry with them. I was always with the fun. But totally I was going to miss it.

I didn't get the beauty of those days when it was running, after it went off, I find its beauty, past days are so beautiful.

When we remember, we get a simple smile on our lips. Only the past is with us to remember.

College never taught us subjects, it taught us how to laugh, how to fight, how to get confident and how to live, how to survive. Only college taught us about life.

'Life with college is good, but life without college is like…?'

After completing college, some went on to coaching and some went for higher education. They had a vision in themselves about career, but mentally they are not and they don't know what to do, to escape from all this they joined in courses and in higher studies.

We were that much addicted to college

After the college, we are all are in touch with each other, but with the fun, with those happy days, we are not in touch. Past life is a memorized life we just take some snaps to memorize.

Memorizing our past is the most memorable feel at present.

The only memorable feel we have at present is memorizing our past.

-¦-¦-¦-

MY MATES WHO MADE MY LITTLE LIFE PRECIOUS

In every college we saw some groups some batches, in our class also some groups were there, but these groups were not rival groups, this was different.

First group;

Ashok, Anil, Ali, Hari Prasad. From the first day onwards they were irregular to college but not to studies. In that I didn't know Hari Prasad by name, I never saw him in the class room, in the first year at the final exam I saw him, and he said, "Arey I also belong to your class."

I saw him and I memorized my past days but I didn't get him, but he was saying that he was my class mate but I didn't recognize him. Who is he wishing me like my class mate? But with a smile I wished him too.

Then he went and sat at his number and then I noticed him.

Hoo roll number 17, every time in class 17 is absent. So he is the seventeen. Ok I got you now. But he said he saw me at class, I don't know when he saw me.

But these fellows were gems in studies, from the first year onwards they were showing their stuff, these fellows completed their subjects at a time, in 'supply' list their numbers were never present, then I understood their capability. These fellows were better than the topper, because the topper is regular to college, and these guys did not have above 60 percent attendance, but still they were completing their semesters.

At college day function we participated in games. We played cricket also, in our team Ashok was the first down player, first time I saw him at the ground. I asked who he is, one of my mate said he is Ashok, our class mate.

Hoo he is Ashok. I had heard his name but I hadn't seen him.

And the rest, Anil and Ali, I saw them at the mid exams; these fellows were a little regular.

At second year also they were the same group. After the second year Subba Reddy also joined with them.

After completing the college all these fellows got jobs before the other fellows.

Another group;

These guys all belonged to the same place, intelligent fellows, they walked together, they ate together and they did everything together. Of them one very interesting fellow, a too jovial fellow, he took lunch with them and in the evening he took snacks with us. Every time he made us laugh. He imitated every one, every lecturer. He was like as his roll number (143) too nasty.

At the farewell day he also cried on the stage. For every one laughter is a good medicine; if we laugh louder our life increases by two minutes. He increased our life every time with his jokes.

And another fellow, he too belongs to the same place but he ate lunch with us and he took snacks with us. He did everything with us, when I got blows during the tour he reacted heavily and he turned a little rebellious on them. But when he got into a fight at the college I just tried to stop, but I didn't react like as him. The next day all my mates blamed us because of my inability. Yes, I did a mistake.

In the second year one of my classmate's mother expired. In the morning while we were moving to college we got the news; my mates stopped the bus and went, but me, I didn't go with them. I went to college. There in college all my classmates heard the news and they got ready to go. And with them I also started out while we were going, this fellow asked me, "Arey you knew about this in the morning, then why didn't you go with them?"

Yes I knew this on the bus; my mates went, but I didn't.

"You are not mature enough to take decisions ra, I mean you didn't get about the situation so you didn't get what to do," he said.

Yes I didn't get about the situation; if we don't react on emotions then we are useless.

By this incident I got my innocence, no, from him I got my innocence.

The only similarity between the two of us is, we both smoke the same brand of cigars.

And about my class girls…

I don't know much about them. Like sketch pens they were also just twelve in the class. Twelve colors, twelve different attitudes, I didn't have enough closeness with them.

So it's better to shut my mouth.

Another idiot

And a very important person in the class, I want to say about him. He made our class complete.

He was from Nandyal, we called him Suri, very nonsense fellow.

Without him our class was empty.

He was just like black color, without black we can't even imagine the other colors. Without him our civil branch was empty of filth and nonsense. His slang and his body language were quite funny.

In the first year in mid exam he came to notice; he didn't know the questions and answers, so he asked the invigilator to change the question paper. In his blunt slang he asked this, and all raised their heads to watch him, and all laughed at his slang. Invigilator was shocked at his question and he didn't accept his request. He went out without writing the exam.

His blunt slang is more attractive in him.

Debate with him is the funniest game with him.

He is a foodie, don't know whether non-veg likes him or he likes non-veg.

This type of fellows we never found in regular. He was a god's gift.

Just simple he is black color in a white paper.

Another person,

Different character, when I was joining in B.Tech, my brother had told me briefly about the attitudes and characters.

Yes, what he said is right at the college we find different characters of friends. When we are at school, we mingle with different attitudes but at that time we don't find differences in them, I think because of our immaturity, but when we get into college we find every character a little surprising. Surely he belongs to that different character.

Till now I didn't get him, and I don't have enough hope in future also.

He is not of our generation. By the mistake of Brahma he joined with us. He is so close to me. He was devotional, he praised all the Gods, his words lead to good.

He is God of our class,

Our class deserves him not only our class every class needs this type character.

Another character

Who was my smoking partner, he only lighted my first cigar.

At the first year he was so regular to college, in the early days so many times he fought for the first bench. When he got out from the bus, he ran into the class room to take the first seat on the first bench, too regular to college. But this did not last for too many days.

This fellow, from second year onwards he forgot the class room, too worse a change. And I had never seen this type of change. Within an year an indigestible change. But he was an intelligent fellow. In the first year I asked my partner about how to make percentage with marks.

He said, "Ok with that."

And I asked how to find marks with percentage.

"Total marks are 700, in that I get 64% then by this percentage how many marks do I get," I asked my partner.

He blurred, he shook his head, and he calculated and gave correct answer but as per mathematics, he can't.

He said, "700 is equal to 100%. In that you get 64%. So 50% is equal to half of the total marks and 1% is equal to seven marks, so for 64% you get 444 marks." this answer I get from him.

All my mates used calculator to get answers but this fellow did not. He gave answers without using calculator and he explained how to me. In every college we can see this type of fellows.

Only roaming on outside from college to Dhaba and Dhaba to college. He spent most of his time in canteen and in Dhaba. I spent most of my time with him.

He was the captain of our cricket team, not only cricket, he played volley ball also. Not only games, along with that he played betting also. He had good fortune in betting.

From our class I hoped that only two fellows would survive in any condition, and in that he was one. But later he fired my hopes.

I ran the whole college with him; sometimes I hated him. Sometimes I worried about him.

Sitting in Dhaba lighting the cigars and nonsense chat is our best time pass. I liked smoking with him.

Three fourth of my days were with him, and I ignored him lots of times also.

After the college he was the only one who got a job within a month. But later he kicked the job. And moved to another.

After the college he made lots of calls to me; out of that, three fourth times I ignored him. He deserves my apologies.

Not only him one of my schoolmates also deserves, he is Pavan. With him also I behaved same but he never ignored me. And he never left from my friendship.

"But sorry is not a good comfortable word between friends."

So no "sorry" for him,

A "good cheer" for him.

Another kid from the mechanical section...

At first he was my bus mate, he was from mechanical. Actually civil guys and mechanical guys are thick friends. We fought with the remaining branches but we never fought with the mechanical guys. All fellows from mechanical were close to me, and in that he was a little close to me. Don't know when he came closer to me. Now he is a little thick to me.

From the 12th standard I am watching this, that after the college education some fellows came close to me; after the 12th standard Rehman came close to me, and now in the B.Tech I think about this character that who was coming close to me after the college.

He is that fellow.

After my graduation he came too close to me.

Another idiot

Roll number 133 was an important number in the class room. Alphabets make dance if I talk about him. Every good and bad kid makes mistakes, in college I also made a mistake that it was I didn't run with him. I missed the enjoyment with him.

In a class every character is important if we miss any character then we miss the sweet recipe of enjoyment.

With these types of characters I completed my engineering.

And a little surprise was still out there.

In the first year I made a pledge, it was that I have to complete my college within four years.

I completed my graduation. At final year 2nd semester, I got 72%.

Hoo I was shocked, I never expected this surprise from the university.

72% for me!

It was a terrible shock for me, I never expected this in B.Tech.

It was a good and big surprise, and more than me, my mom got a heavy shock. All my family members went into shock.

No it was not a shock it was a, it was a surprise for all of them.

But in the aggregate, I got only 64%.

"I completed my B.Tech with 64%."

From school to graduation I am standard in studies, with no change in percentage.

At last I got heavy congratulations from B.Tech.

I finished my graduation.

In engineering I entered with tension, confusion, with fear and with frustrated mind. At the start only dilemmas ran over my mind, but after the engineering I came out with a little confidence. And with a little stuff in hands.

My schooling started with crying, and it ended with crying.

My engineering started with curiosity and it ended with crying.

"In school I was off with sorrow and after graduation I was off with sorrow."

"No change in ending but too different at the beginning."

My 22 years has passed.

I WON'T FEEL ANY SURPRISE,

IF I MISS ANY ONE OF THE INCIDENTS IN MY LIFE"

– Anonymous

"Present never looks beautiful, after it turns to past then we find its beauty."

Memories are beautiful,

And past is so beautiful,

And thinking about the past is too beautiful,